AMERICA IN THE 21ST CENTURY: POLITICAL AND ECONOMIC ISSUES

THE UNITED STATES RESEARCH ENTERPRISE

ENHANCEMENTS FOR THE FUTURE

AMERICA IN THE 21ST CENTURY: POLITICAL AND ECONOMIC ISSUES

Additional books in this series can be found on Nova's website under the Series tab.

Additional E-books in this series can be found on Nova's website under the E-book tab.

AMERICA IN THE 21ST CENTURY: POLITICAL AND ECONOMIC ISSUES

THE UNITED STATES RESEARCH ENTERPRISE

ENHANCEMENTS FOR THE FUTURE

DANIEL S. ROSSER

EDITOR

nova publishers

New York

For permission to use material from this book please contact us:
Telephone 631-231-7269; Fax 631-231-8175
Web Site: http://www.novapublishers.com

Library of Congress Cataloging-in-Publication Data

ISBN: 978-1-62417-916-7

Published by Nova Science Publishers, Inc. † New York

CONTENTS

PREFACE

No country in the history of the world has more readily, or more fruitfully, embraced innovation through science and technology than the United States. The products of our basic and applied scientific research not only provide us with high-quality jobs and support our high-tech and knowledge economies, but they also define us as a nation; as an inventive, entrepreneurial society. The benefits from scientific advances, and the need for such advances to continue, are evident in virtually every aspect of modern life. The United States is in the midst of a profound reorganization of how research is done, where it is done, who does it, and how its results find their way to the marketplace. This confluence of circumstances threatens the Nation's world-leading position in innovation and technology and the benefits it brings. This book examines the importance of what is at stake, and what has been the response to date of the U.S. science and technology enterprise, and discusses the kinds of actions that could create positive opportunities for the United States in the future.

Chapter 1 – The United States is in the midst of a profound reorganization of how research is done, where it is done, who does it, and how its results find their way to the marketplace. This confluence of circumstances threatens the Nation's world-leading position in innovation and technology and the benefits it brings.

As a fraction of its gross domestic product (GDP), U.S. investment in research and development (R&D) used to be first in the world. Today it is eighth (and fourth among large economies). In 2009, Asia's share of total world R&D was about the same as that of the United States. In 2012, Asia will likely surpass the United States' 31-percent share with an estimated 37-percent share. If U.S. willingness to support basic scientific research is undermined by policies that fail to optimally use the fruits of that research to build the U.S.

economy, the United States will in effect cede leadership to other countries. An even worse outcome occurs if other countries, acting without U.S. leadership, make the same mistake, leading to a zero-sum world in which no country invests in long-term basic research for the future, while all scramble to compete over the diminishing returns from past investments.

Such a negative outcome is still avoidable. This report shows how a loss of global competitiveness can be avoided by increasing the productivity of U.S. researchers and by positioning the Nation's great research universities and the National Laboratories as central engines of innovation and geographical anchors of the Nation's science and technology enterprise. The issue is not just quantitative, but qualitative as well. Increased competition, including international competition, is causing U.S. industry to do a smaller share of all basic research. That is, in the R&D spectrum, industry's development ("D") is increasing much faster than its research ("R"). Yet this basic research is the underlying platform on which applied research and engineering development are built. At the same time, other countries' investments in basic and early applied research are increasing. Just as the United States has lost a large portion of its manufacturing to other countries, it is now in danger of losing its advantage in invention and discovery, potentially an even greater calamity.

This PCAST report describes the nature of the current situation, the importance of what is at stake, and what has been the response to date of the U.S. science and technology enterprise. More importantly, it also discusses the kinds of actions that could create positive opportunities for the United States in the face of these troubling trends.

Many of the actions that we recommend in this report reiterate those of other recent discipline-specific PCAST reports. This report thus serves to highlight the crosscutting benefits of such actions and their importance for the entire science and technology enterprise. Actions to improve science, technology, engineering, and math (STEM) education at all levels are prime examples. Likewise, most of our recommendations align with those of recent important studies on the research enterprise by the National Research Council, the American Academy of Arts and Sciences, and others. Both the concordance and the intensity of such studies indicate a strong national consensus that prompt action is needed.

Just as the Nation works to rebuild domestic manufacturing within the United States, and ensure unimpeded access to world markets for its private-sector industry, the Nation must also work to ensure that industry will have immediate, close access to an abundant flow of inventions and discoveries, like those that have always fueled U.S. competitiveness. For this to happen, proactive policies and transformative changes in U.S. educational and research institutions are needed.

Chapter 2 – There is ongoing interest in the pace of U.S. technological advancement due to its influence on U.S. economic growth, productivity, and international competitiveness. Because technology can contribute to economic growth and productivity increases, congressional attention has focused on how to augment private-sector technological development. Legislative activity over the past 30 or more years has created a policy for technology development, albeit an ad hoc one. Because of the lack of consensus on the scope and direction of a national policy, Congress has taken an incremental approach aimed at creating new mechanisms to facilitate technological advancement in particular areas and making changes and improvements as necessary. Congressional action has mandated specific technology development programs and obligations in federal agencies. Many programs were created based upon what individual committees judged appropriate within the agencies over which they had authorization or appropriation responsibilities. However, there has been recent legislative activity directed at eliminating or significantly curtailing many of these federal efforts. Several programs have been terminated and the budgets for other initiatives have declined. The proper role of the federal government in technology development and the competitiveness of U.S. industry continues to be a topic of congressional debate. Legislation affecting the research and development (R&D) environment has included both direct and indirect measures to facilitate technological innovation. In general, direct measures are those which involve budget outlays and the provision of services by government agencies. Indirect measures include financial incentives and legal changes (e.g., liability or regulatory reform; new antitrust arrangements). As the Congress develops its appropriation priorities, the manner by which the government encourages technological progress in the private sector again may be explored and/or redefined.

Chapter 3 – In response to the foreign challenge in the global marketplace, the United States Congress has explored ways to stimulate technological advancement in the private sector. The government has supported various efforts to promote cooperative research and development activities among industry, universities, and the federal R&D establishment designed to increase the competitiveness of American industry and to encourage the generation of new products, processes, and services. Collaborative ventures are intended to accommodate the strengths and responsibilities of all sectors involved in innovation and technology development. Academia, industry, and government often have complementary functions. Joint projects allow for the sharing of costs, risks, facilities, and expertise. Cooperative activity covers various institutional and legal arrangements including industry- industry, industry-university, and industry-government efforts. Proponents of joint ventures argue that they permit work to be done that is too expensive for one company to support and allow for R&D that crosses traditional boundaries of expertise and experience. Such arrangements make use of existing, and support the development of new, resources, facilities, knowledge, and skills. Opponents argue that these endeavors dampen competition necessary for innovation. Federal efforts to encourage cooperative activities include the National Cooperative Research Act; the National Cooperative Production Act; tax changes permitting credits for industry payments to universities for R&D and deductions for contributions of equipment used in academic research; and amendments to the patent laws vesting title to inventions made under federal funding in universities. Technology transfer from the government to the private sector is facilitated by several laws. In addition, there are various ongoing cooperative programs supported by multiple federal departments and agencies. Given the increased popularity of cooperative programs, questions might be raised as to whether they are meeting expectations. Among the issues before Congress are whether joint ventures contribute to industrial competitiveness and what role, if any, the government has in facilitating such arrangements.

In: The United States Research Enterprise
Editor: Daniel S. Rosser
ISBN: 978-1-62417-916-7

Chapter 1

TRANSFORMATION AND OPPORTUNITY: THE FUTURE OF THE U.S. RESEARCH ENTERPRISE*

President's Council of Advisors on Science and Technology

I. EXECUTIVE REPORT

The United States is in the midst of a profound reorganization of how research is done, where it is done, who does it, and how its results find their way to the marketplace. This confluence of circumstances threatens the Nation's world-leading position in innovation and technology and the benefits it brings.

As a fraction of its gross domestic product (GDP), U.S. investment in research and development (R&D) used to be first in the world. Today it is eighth (and fourth among large economies). In 2009, Asia's share of total world R&D was about the same as that of the United States. In 2012, Asia will likely surpass the United States' 31-percent share with an estimated 37-percent share. If U.S. willingness to support basic scientific research is undermined by policies that fail to optimally use the fruits of that research to build the U.S. economy, the United States will in effect cede leadership to other countries.

* This is an edited, reformatted and augmented version of the Executive Office of the President, dated November 2012.

An even worse outcome occurs if other countries, acting without U.S. leadership, make the same mistake, leading to a zero-sum world in which no country invests in long-term basic research for the future, while all scramble to compete over the diminishing returns from past investments.

Such a negative outcome is still avoidable. This report shows how a loss of global competitiveness can be avoided by increasing the productivity of U.S. researchers and by positioning the Nation's great research universities and the National Laboratories as central engines of innovation and geographical anchors of the Nation's science and technology enterprise. The issue is not just quantitative, but qualitative as well. Increased competition, including international competition, is causing U.S. industry to do a smaller share of all basic research. That is, in the R&D spectrum, industry's development ("D") is increasing much faster than its research ("R"). Yet this basic research is the underlying platform on which applied research and engineering development are built. At the same time, other countries' investments in basic and early applied research are increasing. Just as the United States has lost a large portion of its manufacturing to other countries, it is now in danger of losing its advantage in invention and discovery, potentially an even greater calamity.

This PCAST report describes the nature of the current situation, the importance of what is at stake, and what has been the response to date of the U.S. science and technology enterprise. More importantly, it also discusses the kinds of actions that could create positive opportunities for the United States in the face of these troubling trends.

Many of the actions that we recommend in this report reiterate those of other recent discipline-specific PCAST reports. This report thus serves to highlight the crosscutting benefits of such actions and their importance for the entire science and technology enterprise. Actions to improve science, technology, engineering, and math (STEM) education at all levels are prime examples. Likewise, most of our recommendations align with those of recent important studies on the research enterprise by the National Research Council, the American Academy of Arts and Sciences, and others. Both the concordance and the intensity of such studies indicate a strong national consensus that prompt action is needed.

Just as the Nation works to rebuild domestic manufacturing within the United States, and ensure unimpeded access to world markets for its private-sector industry, the Nation must also work to ensure that industry will have immediate, close access to an abundant flow of inventions and discoveries, like those that have always fueled U.S. competitiveness. For this to happen, proactive policies and transformative changes in U.S. educational and research institutions are needed.

1.1. Science and Technology Are Foundational to the American Way of Life

No country in the history of the world has more readily, or more fruitfully, embraced innovation through science and technology than the United States. The products of our basic and applied scientific research not only provide us with high-quality jobs and support our high-tech and knowledge economies, but they also define us as a nation: We are an inventive, entrepreneurial society.

The benefits from scientific advances, and the need for such advances to continue, are evident in virtually every aspect of modern life. We want longer, healthier lives for ourselves, our elder parents, and our children. We want to counter present and future threats to our national security with better technology than that of our adversaries. We want to transform the difficult and complex problems of energy, food, and water supplies, and of protecting the global environment into feasible paths forward.

Americans also want to maintain leadership in areas of scientific and technological inquiry that are not yet directed at known applications or existing global challenges. Some of these areas will later find unexpected practical applications. Others respond to a basic human need to understand the world and mankind's place in it. Popular interest in science and engineering is not limited to immediate or even future applications. Books and television shows about the origin of the universe, or the fundamental nature of matter, or the evolution of life on Earth are perennially in fashion; the public's imagination can be captured by the exploits of a robot vehicle on Mars or by the illimitable thinking of a scientist who is confined to a wheelchair.

Indeed, the U.S. science and technology enterprise mirrors and supports the national character. Americans are both practical and idealistic. From the Yankee watchmaker, through Henry Ford's manufacturing revolution, Bell Laboratories, Xerox PARC, and today's research-intensive corporations, the United States has benefited from the innovative spirit of its industry, a spirit that has impelled Americans to invent things, not just produce them. At the same time, U.S. discoveries in basic research have yielded more than 330 Nobel Prize awards, almost 40 percent of the world's total and more than the next 4 highest countries combined. This duality, to which basic research and practical applications are inextricably linked in a single science and engineering enterprise, is an essential feature of our success and a theme of this report.

Scientific research creates not merely jobs, but high-quality jobs that employ and demand a highly skilled workforce. The educational system that produces such a workforce must go beyond the mere intake of information to challenge the curiosity and character of its students. Some will then go on to create new knowledge, invent, and innovate new products. All can contribute to making a better world. This kind of education, thus, leads not only to immediate excitement and opportunity, but also to higher aspirations and upward economic mobility. The enterprise of scientific research can touch the imagination and idealism of young people and empower them to build a world that strengthens American ideals. The needs of an innovation-based economy provide an incentive for transforming the entire national system of education, from kindergarten through postgraduate education and technical training.

1.2. Research Is a National Investment

Studies of both the U.S. economy over time and of the economies of our economic competitors consistently show that investment in scientific research pays off. Robert Solow's pioneering study (earning him one of the Nobel Prizes mentioned previously) showed that more than half, and perhaps as much as 85 percent of productivity growth in the United States in the first half of the 20th century could be attributed to technical advances. Other studies indicate that 50 percent or more of the nearly sevenfold real growth the country has enjoyed since the end of World War II has been attributable to technological innovation resulting from investments in research and development.

The fact that research provides a healthy return on investment does not alone justify Federal support of all research under all circumstances. In some cases, investment is justified because its returns come in the form of enhancement of public goods (such as national defense, public health and safety, and disaster preparedness) or reduced negative externalities (such as air and water pollution and climate change). In other cases, support is justified by a "market failure" in the private sector whereby the returns from investment in basic and early-stage applied research may not accrue to any one firm or entity that actually pays for the investment. Because the private incentive to undertake basic research is thus attenuated, the private sector will invest too little. If the full social potential is to be realized, the government must compensate by supporting the lion's share of basic research.

Indeed, this was the conclusion reached by Vannevar Bush in his influential report, "Science—the Endless Frontier," submitted to President Harry Truman in July 1945. Bush outlined three basic principles: (1) the Government must be the principal source of funding for basic science; (2) basic science should be located primarily in universities that combine research with the education of the next generation of scientists and engineers; and (3) the Government should allocate funding across broad categories of science, but the decisions to allocate funds to particular projects should be made by independent scientific experts.

The next 50 years witnessed a dramatic rise in Federal support for basic research. It created and drove the university research enterprise. The Federal Government went on to create the National Science Foundation in 1950 and greatly boost funding for the National Institutes of Health. Today, these institutions, along with the newer Department of Energy, remain the primary stewards of basic research in the United States. The partnership between universities and Federal research agencies led to some of the most profound and world-changing discoveries of the 20th century (see Box 1-1).

Vannevar Bush's famous report and the Nation's response to it, "connected the dots" from basic research in science and technology to national prosperity. Experts now recognize that the benefits from research result not just from a linear progression, where basic research in an area leads to applied research, development, and products in that same area. Rather, basic research fuels a whole innovation ecosystem, often in unpredictable ways. Basic research in quantum mechanics and atomic structure, which was curiosity-driven and arcane in its time, later provided the platform on which today's microelectronics and computer industries were built. Basic research in pure mathematics and computer science provided the foundation for many aspects of the World Wide Web, and provided the intellectual foundations for some of today's biggest companies. A similar picture is unfolding today in the biosciences.

The largest returns of research often come from unexpected new discoveries that open up whole new vistas. Such discoveries are often potentiated by a long period of seemingly evolutionary advances. Then, infrequently, but nevertheless with regularity, a particular line of basic research becomes revolutionary with a return that changes the world. Aggregate wealth can rise in giant steps in a world in which new platforms for new industries are regularly, if unexpectedly, created.

Box 1-1. Practical Benefits from Fundamental Research

Practical results that are built on Federally supported fundamental research are virtually everywhere in use. Fundamental break-throughs can be ascribed to the support of many Federal agencies, including National Science Foundation (NSF),[a] Department of Energy (DOE),[b] National Institutes of Health (NIH),[c] National Aeronautics and Space Administration (NASA),[d] U.S. Department of Agriculture (USDA),[e] and the National Oceanic and Atmospheric Administration (NOAA).[f]

While the following examples only scratch the surface, it is worth contemplating how different the world would be without each of these practical benefits of fundamental research.

What would today's world be like without the Internet, modern drugs, computers, wireless telecommunication, passenger jet aircraft, weather satellites, GPS, digital cameras, or the knowledge of the human genome?

The question is fanciful because of the Nation's con-sistent support of fundamental research over the last 60 years. Less fanciful, and subject to legislative and executive decisions, is the question, "What about the next 60 years?"

- The Internet world has grown out of fundamental research: The basic protocols of the Internet were developed by DARPA; the first web server was written for use by international collaborations of high-energy physicists; Google's basic search algorithm came from co-founder Larry Page's Stanford Ph.D. thesis.
- All modern medical imaging technologies rely on the mathematics of inverse problems. Additionally, magnetic resonance imaging (MRI) uses properties of the atomic nucleus originally studied to understand quantum mechanics, an approach first exploited by radio astronomers, and superconducting magnets that are commercial versions of magnets originally built for particle physics accelerators.
- Weather satellites, ground-based Doppler radar, and computer modeling on supercomputers produce vastly more accurate weather forecasts than were possible a generation or two ago, benefitting public safety and agriculture and providing daily convenience.

- The Human Genome Project, whose benefits include new cancer therapies, personalized medicine, and DNA forensic identification, began as a fundamental research partnership between DOE and NIH.
- The wings of all airplanes designed since World War II owe their effectiveness to research by National Advisory Committee for Aeronautics (the predecessor agency to NASA) and, more recently, to developments in computational fluid dynamics at U.S. National Laboratories.
- The development of database technologies that today underlie virtually all commerce depended on many exchanges between researchers in academia (notably the University of California, Berkeley, and the University Wisconsin) and industry (notably IBM and later Oracle).
- The laser and its predecessor the maser (the technology behind GPS) were invented in a fertile combination of cooperation and competition among universities (especially Columbia and Stanford) and corporate laboratories (Bell and Hughes).
- Nanotechnology research, on the heels of coordinated Federal investment, is leading to advances in areas such as new drug delivery systems, more resilient materials and fabrics, safer and more effective industrial catalysts, faster computer chips, and sustainable development in water and energy resources.
- Cortisone and other medical steroids became affordable in the 1950s only after USDA and NIH researchers discovered a chemical precursor in a wild Mexican yam. Subsequent research in the private sector led to the development of oral contraceptives and many other drugs.
- Lithiumion batteries, ubiquitous in cellphones and computers, depend on basic discoveries at State University of New York (SUNY) Binghamton in the 1970s, Bell Labs in the 1980s, and MIT in the 2000s. Technology for the larger lithium batteries used in hybrid and electric cars was developed at Lawrence Berkeley National Laboratory.
- Charge-coupled devices (CCDs) that record the images in all of today's digital cameras and cell phones were a product of fundamental research at Bell Labs in the 1960s.

- Bar codes, and more recently Quick Response (QR) codes recognizable by cell-phone cameras, grew out of basic research in computer vision and the pure mathematics of error-correcting codes.
- Basic research performed using synchrotron light sources at U.S. National Laboratories has resulted in at least three Nobel prizes for work in biomedical research.

References:
[a] "NSF Sensational 60" at www.nsf.gov/about/history
[b] DOE, "Technology Transfer Program Successes" at techtransfer.energy.gov/success/techtranstories.pdf
[c] "NIH Technologies in the Development of Healthcare Products" at /www.ott.nih.gov/pdfs/techdev.pdf.
[d] NASA Office of the Chief Technologist, "Success Stories" at www.nasa.gov/offices/oct/success/index.html.
[e] USDA Agricultural Research Service, "Technologies in the Marketplace" at www.ars.usda.gov/business/docs.htm?docid=769.
[f] NOAA, Office of Research and Technology Applications at www.oar.noaa.gov/orta/.

The response to the Vannevar Bush report was not the first time that the Federal Government and universities had partnered to meet a critical national need for research. Nearly a century earlier, the areas of great national need were agriculture, mechanical arts, and home economics. The Morrill Act of 1862 created the Land Grant Colleges to provide, in each state of the union, education in these crucial areas. Beyond their education responsibilities, faculty members were further expected to conduct research in these areas of need and share the results of this research with the surrounding communities through outreach programs. The second Morrill Act in 1890 secured these foundational benefits of education for all U.S. citizens.

Today's challenges resemble a combination of these two previous episodes, embodying a kind of perfect storm. On one hand, the United States needs to protect its ability to generate foundational basic research, as the Vannevar Bush report emphasized. On the other hand, much more needs to be done to enable the fruits of that research to become platforms for products, jobs, and new industries, as the Morrill Act did for the agriculture enterprise. The underlying question that this report seeks to address is: How can the United States best pursue these two goals simultaneously?

1.3. A Global Reorganization of Research Is Happening

In a globalized economy, international competition in the private sector drives structural changes in national economies. If the competitive playing field is level, these changes create greater global economic efficiency and, at least in the short run, greater overall wealth. However, they also have consequences that can affect the trajectories of nations in ways other than economic.

In the global economy, companies that traditionally capitalized on regional U.S. markets must now compete against organizations all over the world. The speed with which products and services can be delivered around the world, from almost anywhere to almost anywhere, diminishes the home-field advantage that used to shield local companies against foreign competitors.

When no single business can capture all the economic benefits that come from a new product, technology, or way of doing business, corporations with obligations to shareholders will tend to underinvest in innovation. When international competition is fierce, private firms will be more interested in R&D investments that give them an immediate competitive advantage and therefore will choose to invest preferentially in low-risk endeavors—those closer to the development and implementation end of the spectrum.

This aspect of globalization has hit basic research done by industry particularly hard. Beginning with the rapid expansion of global competition in the 1990s and the new focus on shareholder value, support by U.S. industry for basic and early applied research (i.e., research with more than a 3-to-5 year time horizon) has stagnated relative to investments in short-term development and also relative to the basic research investments of some of our international competitors.

The great industrial centers of basic research, such as Bell Labs and RCA Labs, flourished in times very different from now. Regulated monopolies, or stable consumer brand preferences, gave these companies strong, predictable cash flows. They were able to take risks, despite the uncertainty of translating basic research into new products. Since the 1990s, the industrial landscape has changed, however. Predictable cash flows and regulated monopolies are largely things of the past, meaning that companies today are far less able to take a long-term view.

Globalization also allows U.S. corporations to perform many aspects of R&D more cost-effectively offshore. Not only is the cost of offshore skilled workers often lower, but the availability of such workers (e.g., trained scientists and engineers) is often higher. The relatively small number of U.S. college graduates with STEM education is a large contributing factor, as is also the scarcity of STEM-enabled technicians with post-secondary certification other than college degrees. Moving R&D offshore is a rational economic choice for the companies themselves, but it has negative long-term consequences for the United States, even when compensated by R&D flows in the other direction.

The United States today has fewer and smaller corporate laboratories than it did just a generation ago. Research by industry now focuses more on development and less on basic and applied research; industry supports a much smaller fraction of basic research than it once did. Fundamental research done with no specific application in mind has especially diminished. As R&D increasingly migrates offshore, it is becoming clear that, unless we act, innovation, in the long run closely paired with production, could migrate with it.

1.4. Universities Are Becoming Central Hubs of the Innovation Ecosystem

The United States has the world's greatest research universities. According to an annual ranking by *The Times* of London, we have 7 of the top 10 and 18 of the top 25 institutions.

With the decline of investment in research by industry and specialized research laboratories, U.S. research universities are today performing not only the basic research for which they have been best known during the last 50 years, but to an increasing extent applied and translational research with the potential to deliver innovations, new industries, and market efficiencies over the next 50 years. Today, American research universities are closer to the marketplace than they have ever been, with a focus on translating and transferring research discoveries to industry.

Universities, along with our National Laboratories (themselves unique in the world for range and quality) are also increasingly hubs of research for national needs such as national security, health, and environmental stewardship. In earlier decades, domestic corporate laboratories such as Bell Labs, could be tapped by government as needs arose. That era is gone.

As industry works with universities as a key source of innovation, the type of research they are funding has evolved. In addition to funding some basic research, industry increasingly funds applied projects to solve specific technical issues. While industry-industry relationships remain common, industry increasingly turns to academia for research partnerships, exposure to leading-edge thinking and technology, objective advice on strategic decision-making, and recruitment of skilled employees with fresh perspectives and state-of-the-art knowledge who can become future company leaders.

1.5. Actions Are Needed to Preserve the U.S. Innovation Advantage

Times of transformation are also times of opportunity. In the main text of this report, we recommend a series of actions that follow from what we see as five key opportunities:

- Key Opportunity #1. The Nation has the opportunity to maintain its world-leading position in R&D investment, structured as a mutually supporting partnership among industry, the Federal Government, universities, and other governmental and private entities.
- Key Opportunity #2. The Federal Government has the opportunity to enhance its role as the enduring foundational investor in basic and early applied research in the United States. It can adopt policies that are most consistent with that role. Federal policy can seek to foster a sustainable R&D enterprise in which, when research is deemed worth supporting, it is supported for success.
- Key Opportunity #3. Federal agencies have the opportunity to grow portfolios that more strategically support a mix of evolutionary vs. revolutionary research; disciplinary vs. interdisciplinary work; and project-based vs. people-based awards.
- Key Opportunity #4. There is the opportunity for government to create additional policy encouragements and incentives for industry to invest in research, both on its own and in new partnerships with universities and the National Laboratories.
- Key Opportunity #5. Research universities have the opportunity to strengthen and enhance their additional role as hubs of the innovation ecosystem. While maintaining the intellectual depth of their foundations in basic research, they can change their educational programs to better prepare their graduates to work in today's world. They can become more proactive in transferring research results into the private sector.

The table in Section 1.7 summarizes the sets of actions that we discuss and recommend in support of each key opportunity. Full discussion of each action is in the main text. However, a few of the more important ones deserve mention here.

(Action #1.1) PCAST recommends reaffirming the President's goal that total R&D expenditures should achieve and sustain a level of 3 percent of GDP. Congressional authorization committees should take ownership of pieces of that goal, with the Executive Branch and Congress establishing policies to enhance private industry's major share.

(Action #1.2) Recognizing the inherent political difficulty, PCAST nevertheless urges Congress and the Executive Branch to find one or more mechanisms for increasing the stability and predictability of Federal research funding, including funding for research infrastructure and facilities. Possibilities include a cross-agency multiyear program and financial plan akin to Department of Defense's (DoD) Future Years Defense Program (FYDP) or closer coupling of multiyear authorizations to actual appropriations for R&D.

(Action #1.3) The Research and Experimentation Tax Credit (usually called the R&D tax credit) needs to be made permanent. An increase in the rate of the alternative simplified credit from 14 percent to 20 percent would not be excessive. The credit also needs to be made more useful to small and medium enterprises that are R&D intensive by instituting any or all of (1) refundable tax credits, (2) transferable tax credits, or (3) modifications in the definition of net operating loss to give advantage to R&D expenditures.

(Action #2.1) Regulatory and policy reform regarding universities is needed and should be spearheaded by the Office of Management and Budget (OMB) and Office of Science and Technology Policy (OSTP). Building on efforts already initiated by the Administration, regulations and policies which do not add value or enhance accountability should be eliminated. There is a remarkable consensus among stakeholders inside and outside government about how to proceed, and significant progress is within reach.

(Action #3.1) Each agency should have a strategic plan that explicitly addresses the different kinds of research activities that can contribute to its mission, specifically addressing the axes of evolutionary vs. revolutionary research, disciplinary vs. interdisciplinary work, and project-based vs. people-based awards. The elements of such plans should be explicitly supported by different kinds of merit review mechanisms (Action #3.2).

(Action #4.1 and #5.2) The quality of undergraduate STEM education is not what it needs to be. Universities have the opportunity to share and adopt best practices, including teaching methods that have been empirically validated. Undergraduate STEM majors should have the opportunity to experience the creation of new knowledge through authentic research experiences. Improvements in undergraduate STEM education will involve the engagement of leaders across academia, disciplinary societies, foundations, and private industry, along with local, state, and Federal governments. We endorse the recommendations of PCAST's recent "Engage to Excel" report.

(Action #4.2) We need to attract and retain, both for universities and industry, the world's best researchers and students from abroad. Federal policies must support these goals by, for example, giving STEM graduates from accredited U.S. universities a fast-tracked, long-term visa, increasing the number of H-1B visas, and/or allowing existing visas to cover an employee's spouse and children.

1.6. Guide to the Report

Chapter 2 further discusses economic and non-economic cases for maintaining a robust U.S. science and technology enterprise and the reasons that basic and early applied research must be primarily Federally supported. Chapter 3 gives a more detailed analysis of the global reorganization of research that is happening today, looks at what national assets can be brought to bear on this transformation, and discusses how these assets are already (if often piecemeal and without an overall strategy) being redeployed.

Chapters 4, 5, and 6 address our five key opportunities and the sets of recommended actions that support each. Chapter 4 discusses key actions that are needed to maintain U.S. R&D leadership, including some reshaping of the role of the Federal Government as sponsor of research. Chapter 5 addresses how the policy environment can be improved for research and innovation in industry. Chapter 6 discusses the kinds of best practices that can be adopted by research universities in their new role as hubs of the innovation ecosystem, responsible both for creating new basic knowledge and for, with increased efficacy, coupling it to the private sector.

Chapter 7 reiterates and summarizes the five key opportunities and the recommended sets of supporting actions and also discusses the concordance between PCAST's recommendations and those of other recent influential reports.

1.7. Summary of Key Opportunities and Supporting Sets of Actions

PCASTS "Transformation and Opportunity" Key Opportunities and Supporting Sets of Actions

Key Opportunities	Supporting Sets of Actions (Details in Main Text)
#1. The Nation has the opportunity to maintain its world-leading position in research investment, structured as a mutually supporting partnership among industry, the Federal Government, universities, and other governmental and private entities.	#1.1. Reaffirm the President's goal that total R&D expenditures should achieve and sustain a level of 3 percent of GDP. Congressional authorization committees should take ownership of pieces of that goal, with the Executive Branch and Congress establishing policies to enhance private industry's major share. (Section 4.1) #1.2. Recognizing the inherent political difficulty, we nevertheless urge Congress and the Executive Branch to find one or more mechanisms for increasing the stability and predictability of Federal research funding, including funding for research infrastructure and facilities. Possibilities include a cross-agency, multiyear program and financial plan akin to DoD's Future Years Defense Program (FYDP) or closer coupling of multiyear authorizations to actual appropriations for R&D. (Section 4.1) #1.3. The R&D tax credit needs to be made permanent. An increase in the rate of the alternative simplified credit from 14 percent to 20 percent would not be excessive. The credit also needs to be made more useful to small and medium enterprises that are R&D intensive by instituting any or all of (1) refundable tax credits, (2) transferable tax credits, or (3) modifications in the definition of net operating loss to give advantage to R&D expenditures. (Section 4.2) #1.4. Adopt policies that increase the productivity of researchers, including more people-based awards, larger and longer awards for some merit-selected investigators, and administratively efficient grant mechanisms. (Section 4.3)
#2. The Federal Government has the opportunity to enhance its role as the enduring foundational investor in basic and early applied research in the United States. It can adopt policies that are most consistent with that role. Federal policy can seek to foster a sustainable R&D enterprise in which, when research is deemed worth supporting, it is supported for success.	#2.1. Identify and achieve regulatory policy reforms, particularly relating to the regulatory burdens on research universities. (Section 4.4) • The Association of American Universities-Association of Public and Land-grant Universities-Council on Governmental Relations (AAU-APLU-COGR) consensus list deserves attention #2.2. Appropriately circumscribe the use of cost sharing by funding agencies. (Section 4.4) • Apply 2009 NSF reforms Federal Government-wide

Key Opportunities	Supporting Sets of Actions (Details in Main Text)
#3. Federal agencies have the opportunity to grow portfolios that more strategically support a mix of evolutionary vs. revolutionary research; disciplinary vs. interdisciplinary work; and project-based vs. people-based awards.	#3.1. Each agency should have a strategic plan that explicitly addresses the different kinds of research activities that can contribute to its mission, specifically addressing the axes of evolutionary vs. revolutionary research; disciplinary vs. interdisciplinary work; and project-based vs. people-based awards. (Section 4.5) #3.2. Each agency should diversify its mechanisms for merit review so as to be optimal for the portfolio in its strategic plan. (Section 4.5) #3.3. Each agency should adopt policies that increase the agility of funding new fields, unexpected opportunities, and the creativity of new researchers. (Section 4.5) • Fellowships (including portable) and training grants • Early career opportunities
#4. There is the opportunity for government to create additional policy encouragements and incentives for industry to invest in research, both on its own and in new partnerships with universities and the National Laboratories.	#4.1. Improve STEM education so as to produce more and better home-grown researchers and technology entrepreneurs. (Section 5.1) • Two previous PCAST reports recommend policy directions #4.2. Attract and retain, both for universities and industry, the world's best researchers and students from abroad. (Section 5.1) • Visa reform for high-ability STEM graduates #4.3. Support the President's Export Control Reform initiative and further measures. (Section 5.2) • Reduce "deemed export" burdens on universities • Unleash U.S. firms to compete internationally #4.4. Enable streamlined interactions between U.S. National Laboratories and industry. (Section 5.3)
#5. Research universities have the opportunity to strengthen and enhance their additional role as hubs of the innovation eco-system. While maintaining the intellectual depth of their foundations in basic research, they can change their educational programs to better prepare their graduates to work in today's world. They can become more proactive in transferring research results into the private sector.	#5.1. Maintain strong commitment to the scope and intellectual depth of fundamental university research. (Section 6.1) • Fundamental research provides the foundation for future world-changing new industries #5.2. Augment the educational mission for today's world. (Section 6.2) • Train for entrepreneurship and technology transfer • Prepare for national needs and grand challenges • Increase undergraduate research experiences #5.3. Embrace more fully the additional role of universities as hubs of the innovation ecosystem. (Section 6.3) • Technology licensing best practices • Proof-of-concept centers • Leadership in public-private partnerships #5.4. Confront difficult career-development and workforce issues, including length of time to Ph.D. and the reliance of the S&T enterprise on the labor of early career training positions. (Section 6.4)

II. Science and Technology Are Central to U.S. World Leadership

Twentieth-century American innovation was breathtaking in its scope and achievements: the ending of World War II and the Cold War; the control of polio; the development of high-yield crops; the increase in life expectancy by more than 50 percent; the decrease in death rates from heart disease, stroke, tuberculosis, and HIV; the invention of the transistor, the laser, the accelerator, and the personal computer; the human and robotic exploration of space; new materials like Kevlar and Teflon; the rise of the Internet and the remarkable growth and dominance of the United States economy. All of these achievements were driven in part or in whole by American innovations in science and technology. The foundation for these successes stemmed from a vision, formulated in the World War II era, of the importance of the U.S. science and technology enterprise to the future of national security, health, and jobs[1]—and from the commitment and coordinated actions taken to realize this vision. This report will address the future of the U.S. science and technology research enterprise. In this report, the scope of the research enterprise includes the following:

- Fundamental or basic research driven largely by the pursuit of knowledge.
- Early applied research more closely aligned with applications, but not yet ripe to be commercialized.
- Later applied (or translational) research, the intellectual feedstock of the private sector.[2]

When the scope expands from research to research and development (R&D), additional activities are essential:

- Engineering research and development to create and realize products.
- Deployment and maturation of manufacturing and distribution technologies.

The central focus of this report is the role of the Federal Government in stewarding and supporting the research enterprise. Our emphasis is on basic and early applied research, on the processes by which such research can be brought to the point of commercialization, and on the essential role of Federal policy and investment in enabling and enhancing such research. Since American universities are not only major contributors to scientific research, but also the principal developers of human talent, much of our focus is on them. However, the private sector contributes two-thirds of U.S. expenditures on research and development, especially development. Thus, the economic value of universities' research accomplishments can benefit the Nation only insofar as these accomplishments are effectively coupled to the needs of a strong private sector. So the second focus of this report is on how that coupling can be made more effective, both by actions of the universities and the private sector and by appropriate Federal policies pertaining to regulation, incentives, and partnerships. In each area addressed, the main attributes of the present state will be examined and recommendations to guide the Federal role into the future will be provided, along with recommendations for the academic and private sectors.

2.1. Science and Technology Are Foundational to the American Way of Life

No country in the history of the world has more readily, or more fruitfully, embraced innovation through science and technology than the United States. The products of our Nation's basic and applied scientific research not only provide us with high-quality jobs and support our high-tech and knowledge economies, but they also define us as a Nation – to ourselves and to the world. In this section, we discuss these broader benefits of science to the American people. In two sections after this one, we examine the more technical economic case, supported by a large body of research, for government support of basic and applied research, not just as a defining social value but also as a high-return investment.

Science and the American National Character

Science in part defines what America wants to be in the world: an inventive, entrepreneurial society. America's unique place in the world is not conferred by a one-time historical grant. It is built on and renewed by the hard work and innovation of every generation. Science is ingrained in the national characteristics of innovation, exploration, discovery, and hard work. The drive to understand our place on this planet and within the universe is a trait that defines our humanity.

A society that devotes some of its best minds to science and research states explicitly that it is committed to the future and to a better, more prosperous world. History has left little doubt that the fruits of research and technology, if managed properly, can lead to just such a world. One can only imagine a world without the technological benefits that were realized in the last century. But beyond such benefits, science and research also speak to the national character. They are indicators that facts and proof actually matter, that ideas are strengthened by the unfettered discourse among peers, and that justice is based not on rhetoric but on conclusions drawn from fact and reason. In short, science, as the word's Latin origin *to know* implies,[3] is the evidence that a society is committed to judgments and actions that are based on knowledge. It is the evidence of a commitment to a better world not driven only by individual self-interest but also by a desire to pool talents and discoveries that promote the general welfare.

Health and Medicine for Healthier, Longer Lives

While the benefits from scientific advancements are evident in virtually every aspect of modern life, they are perhaps most immediate in the area of human health. Biological discoveries have lengthened our lives; in the mid-2000s, the life expectancy in the United States reached an all-time high of 77.5 years, up from 49.2 years at the beginning of the twentieth century.[4] Advances in treatment rooted in improved understanding of biological function contribute to continual improvements in the quality of life in later years. HIV-AIDS, whose diagnosis was once a death sentence; is now treatable: In areas where HAART (highly active anti-retroviral therapy) became available, deaths related to HIV have decreased by 94 percent[5] and transmission rates by 96 percent.6 Thanks to the development of vaccines, global incidences of diseases, including diphtheria, polio, yellow fever, and tetanus, have plummeted, and smallpox has been eradicated. Sequencing of the human genome has led to the identification of genes associated with diseases such as multiple sclerosis and cystic fibrosis, bringing the promise of improved treatment and ultimately a cure.

A healthier population is also an economically more productive population.[7] That is not, however, the only reason that Americans value the benefits of biomedical research. We want longer, healthier lives for our elder parents, ourselves, and our children. Further, it is an American social value to be generous in bringing healthier lives to our own neediest and to the world. Today, Americans look to science and technology for health care that is not only more effective, but also more affordable, so that all may benefit fully.

National and Homeland Security

Science has been, and will continue to be, crucial in maintaining the Nation's security. Advances rooted in the physical sciences, such as the discovery of radar, which helped win World War II; the development of infrared observation used on the battlefield; and methods of precise targeting and orbital reconnaissance, have been central to U.S. national security and defense. While national security depends on the effectiveness of such technologies, it also depends on the ability of these systems to deter aggressors or ideological adversaries. We value strong national security in part so as to make military conflict rarer. In most cases, superior technology is derived from a strong and enduring investment in fundamental research. A strong foundation in research allows important applications not just in the areas in which the research is focused, but in numerous related areas as well. This compounding of benefits exemplifies the mutual reinforcement of the diverse, interrelated, and interdependent fields of modern science.

Technological prowess built on a strong research foundation is not only a key element of both deterrence and actual conflict, but it is also enormously important to the confidence of American citizens. Future threats may increasingly arise from non-state actors and asymmetrical warfare, requiring different kinds of technology innovations and responses. The recent effectiveness of unmanned aerial vehicles against terrorism threats provides one example. The national mood is highly dependent on ensuring that the Nation cannot be "out-thought" or "out-innovated" by an adversary. Americans want to minimize the possibility of being endangered by technological surprise.

Support for national security is deep and broad across the American political spectrum. But this does not mean that the country can afford an unlimited budget for defense. Science and engineering research provide the crucial leverage for the United States to stay ahead of current and future adversaries by brains and technology as the alternative to massive military interventions. For example, research in the biological sciences is required to thwart or respond to new threats from bioterrorism. Unless defended against, cyber warfare could come to threaten U.S. physical, economic, and virtual infrastructures, and it could be used as a coercive threat in world affairs. When interventions prove necessary, advanced technologies are key to minimizing casualties, far fewer than could have been imagined in previous warfare.

Support for national security also depends on what economists call "non-substitutable outcomes." World history is full of examples of nations and civilizations that, while wealthy economically, were eventually brought down by forces or events for which they were not prepared. Economic security is one contributor to national security, but it must be augmented by other kinds of soft, hard, and "smart" power.[8] A nation whose strengths are based not only on wealth, but also on knowledge, especially including a domestic base for technological innovation, is more resilient and flexible in the face of unforeseeable world events, including economic, environmental, and political crises. Science and engineering research that is both strong today and capable of addressing national needs in the future provides an essential reserve of national security. The power of research rests on its ability to open up the solution space for future crises not yet envisioned.

Resiliency in an Uncertain World

As we look to the future, a number of grand challenges demand the Nation's attention, including limited food supply, threat of pandemic disease, unequal access to health care, terrorism, energy supplies, climate change, and nuclear war. Each of these challenges is complex. None will be solved by actions that are now clearly defined. The mistaken deployment of an inappropriate technology or an ineffective one could bring unexpected harm. As a Nation, we must prepare individuals and develop institutions sufficiently resilient to confront such issues and to address unanticipated events with flexibility. Such resiliency demands a strong commitment to people who exhibit the insight and strength to face the unknown—and thus to research.

To act effectively in the face of uncertainty, the Nation must maintain the belief that discovery can transform an impossible problem into a solvable one. The discovery of the transistor has transformed modern diagnostic medicine, communication, and weather forecasting—all in unexpected ways. Future discoveries to confront, if not resolve, the next great challenges are best enabled by supporting the free range of curious minds to build a strong foundation on which to innovate.

Protecting the Planet and Feeding Humanity

Economic and societal well-being depend on the sustainability of environmental capital—the planet's ecosystems and the biodiversity they contain. The Nation must improve its ability to protect people and ecosystems simultaneously. As a case in point, short-term weather prediction has improved markedly, as evidenced by advanced path-predicting technology allowing for preparedness along the East Coast during Hurricane Irene in 2011.[9] During the same year, predictions of the timing and intensity of recent tornadoes in Alabama and Georgia enabled early warnings that minimized loss of life, although much more progress is required to understand severe storms.

Among the most crucial problems faced by humans is the availability of ample food and clean water. Continually improving crop yields will be required to meet the increased demand of a growing population[10] and changing climate.[11] Similarly, while the safety of the U.S. water supply has long been a central concern of public health, many challenges remain in providing a sufficient quantity of high-quality water to much of the Nation and the world.[12]

The Value of Discovery-Driven Science

Some areas of scientific inquiry are not directed at known applications or societal needs, but still provide great value to society. When Galileo's detailed observations demonstrated beyond doubt that the Earth was part of a heliocentric solar system, he triggered a scientific revolution that changed humanity's view of its place in the universe. The desire to understand the world and our place in it drives much of the most exciting science. Astronomers and physicists use the most complex instruments ever built to explore the nature of the dark matter and dark energy that make up most of the universe. Mathematicians are experiencing a golden age, solving problems that have resisted solution for decades or centuries[13] and opening up new ways to think about the physical world. Archaeologists and geneticists employ very different but equally sophisticated techniques to determine how humans emerged from Africa to populate the planet. Nothing is more human than the drive to understand human origins, and nothing does more to elevate the human spirit.

Discovery-driven science may also lead to eventual applications of great value that could not have been foreseen during the early, foundational research. An understanding of Einstein's beautiful theory of general relativity is essential to the global positioning system (GPS). Accelerator technology, developed to understand quarks and leptons, led to synchrotron light sources that have revolutionized the process of creating new drugs.[14] No diagram of the R&D process can capture the numerous ways in which such science can transform technology and society.

Finally, the very unfolding and story of science, the excitement of a Nobel-prize winner and her astonishing discovery, often serves to draw the young researcher into a career. Once inspired by a narrative of discovery, inquisitive and inventive new scientists often go on to solve the grand technical challenges that pique their curiosity.

Education About Science Strengthens Democracy

The essence of a democracy in modern society is best seen in its commitment to provide educational opportunities to its people. This commitment requires educational opportunity that goes beyond the essentials of life, challenging the curiosity and character of its people to make a better world. Such a forward-pressing education is possible only when strong scientific research is a vital part of the institutions and individuals that educate and inspire. Education that is not continually enriched by the freedom of research and ever-deepening understandings will fade into an uninspiring endeavor of imposed ideas and outdated concepts.

The healthy research enterprise touches the idealism of young people and empowers them to build a world that ultimately strengthens democracy. The logical reasoning and critical thinking at the base of scientific and technological discovery ultimately lead to informed decision-making. Having sufficient technical training to understand threats to health, security, the environment, and energy sources underpins responsible citizenship. Scientific research creates not merely jobs, but high-quality jobs that employ and demand a highly skilled workforce. Thus, the path of education leads not only to excitement and opportunity, but also to upward economic mobility and to a voting citizenry capable of critical thinking.

In his first annual address to the first Congress, George Washington wrote, "There is nothing which can better deserve your patronage than the promotion of science and literature. Knowledge is, in every country, the surest basis of public happiness."[15]

2.2. The Direct Economic Benefits of Research Are Substantial

Research Investments Fuel Economic Growth

According to a 2009 Pew poll, a large majority of Americans think that government investments in basic scientific research (73 percent) and engineering and technology (74 percent) pay off in the long run, with only small differences between Democrats and Republicans reported.[16]

This intuitive belief is well-supported by studies of both the U.S. economy and of its competitors over time. Robert Solow's pioneering study, earning him a Nobel Prize, showed that more than half, and perhaps as much as 85 percent, of productivity growth in the United States in the first half of the 20th century could be attributed to technical advances.[17] Between 2000 and 2007, more than two-thirds of productivity growth in the United Kingdom (UK) was the result of innovation.[18] Many other comparable results are cited in recent public reports.[19]

Federal Support of Research Responds to a Well-Understood Market Failure

The fact that research provides a healthy return on investment does not justify Federal support of all research under all circumstances. In the previously cited Pew poll, some Americans (29 percent) held the view that private investment could ensure enough scientific progress without government intervention. What is the evidence to support this view, and how should it affect the way we think about Federal support of basic and early applied research?

In purely economic terms, Federal support of basic and early applied research is justified by the economic concept of market failure. Here, the so-called failure is not that research fails to produce direct returns on investment. It is that those returns may not accrue to (economists say "be appropriable by") any one firm or entity that actually pays for the investment. In terms first popularized by Kenneth Arrow, the knowledge products of basic scientific research are "non-rival" and "non-excludable."[20] That is, any number of people can profit from an advance in basic scientific knowledge; and no one can be stopped from profiting from it. In this context, scientific discovery is a public good that benefits all. Because the private incentive to undertake basic research is thus attenuated, the private sector will tend to invest too little, and if the full social potential is to be realized, the government must compensate by supporting the lion's share of basic research.[21]

In 1995, Griliches[22] reviewed studies spanning over 30 years that estimated both the private (appropriable) return and the social return (the sum of the benefits accruing to the investor and to others) for investments in research and development. Social benefits include the growth of the economy, the creation of new and better jobs, and improvements to the environment. In virtually every study, the returns were large. For appropriable returns, most of the estimates were in the range of 20–50 percent per year. For total returns, including non-appropriable, they were even higher, most in the range 50–80 percent per year.[23] If these figures were truly attainable today by U.S. firms as *appropriable* returns from investments in basic and early applied research, then perhaps Federal funding of research would not be necessary after all.

Unfortunately, however, these figures combine returns on research *and development*, the two being difficult to separate statistically in these kinds of analyses. While the development ("D") in R&D cannot proceed without the research ("R"), it is the development that produces most of the appropriable returns, while the research generates most, if not all, the non-appropriable returns. Studies that have attempted to measure returns from publicly funded R&D, by its nature mostly "R", have found large (non-appropriable) rates of return; but such measurements are difficult.[24] Whether public investment in basic research supplants investments that might have been made by industry is likewise inconclusive in empirical data.[25] On balance, however, it seems likely to most observers that direct, appropriable returns from basic and early applied research remain too small to garner sufficient private capital and can be adequately supported only by government.[26]

What the large returns found in Griliches' study and more recent ones[27] strongly support is the belief that large appropriable returns accrue to individual U.S. firms that invest in R&D—and even larger non-appropriable returns accrue to the U.S. public—but only when there is Federal investment in the public good of basic and early applied research.[28] As an example of the wisdom of common sense, this is concordant with the beliefs of the Pew poll's large majority of Americans.

In a Competitive, Globalized Economy, Federal Policies on Research Support Matter More

Many of the same considerations that affect the willingness of firms to invest in basic research also affect the willingness of nations to invest. A nation's willingness to invest depends on whether its returns (now including as appropriable the social returns that benefit its citizens) are sufficient to justify the investment and are a better investment than competing priorities. Put bluntly, the U.S. taxpayer's enthusiasm for investments in research might be different if the returns on such investment flowed dominantly to competitor nations, with little return to the United States.

In 1945, when the U.S. share of world GDP is estimated to have been about 50 percent, and when few countries in the world had the necessary technical and manufacturing infrastructure to capitalize on U.S. scientific discoveries, there was little doubt that the economic returns of U.S. investments in basic research would be dominantly appropriable by the United States. Then, scientific knowledge was transmitted by paper journals that crossed the world's oceans by freighter, and only a small fraction of U.S. graduate students in the sciences were from other countries. In his famous report to President Truman, Vannevar Bush took as a given that the benefits of U.S. "scientific capital" would flow dominantly to the United States.[29]

Today, the U.S. fraction of world GDP is below 25 percent.[30] Many countries in Europe and Asia have the ability to commercialize scientific discoveries made in the United States—as the United States has the ability to commercialize discoveries made abroad.[31] Scientific knowledge flows at the speed of the Internet. Foreign students, now making up 28 percent[32] of U.S. graduate enrollments in the sciences and engineering, are both a rich source of talent for the United States and its industries and also a conduit for further global leveling of the scientific playing field. All these factors act to lower the immediate appropriability of U.S. investment in basic research. But the same factors offer new opportunities for the United States to benefit from research supported by other nations, as well as from multinational research collaborations. Where once the United States was alone at the pinnacle of creative scientific discovery, that summit is increasingly accessible to researchers of other nations. Scientific discovery is not a zero-sum game: a rising tide can lift all boats. However, there is little doubt that economic competition in the world today is more intense than it was a half century ago.

With specific regard to the United States, some sectors of the current economy have been stagnant since the 2008 market crash, and the current state of affairs presents a fundamental structural issue for the country. Recovery of the economy in the long term will require genuine growth, to which research and development must be a major contributor. As a country, the Nation has moved from an era in which the appropriability, and therefore economic benefit, of investment in research was beyond question to an era in which what benefit there is depends on our having the right policies for *how* we as a Nation invest in research, and *what we do* to ensure that the fair share of its benefits accrue to the U.S. economy. The Government needs to act wisely, both independently and also in a shared-leadership role with other countries, so that (1) it is in the self-interest of many nations, including the United States, to make significant investments in basic and applied research, and (2) all nations, including the United States, benefit economically from the others' investments. A recent study by the National Academies[33] discusses the emerging policies of six nations (China, Japan, India, Brazil, Russia, and Singapore) in this regard.

The stakes are high. If U.S. willingness to support basic scientific research is undermined by policies that fail to optimally use the fruits of that research to build the U.S. economy, the United States will in effect cede leadership and appropriability of returns to other countries. An even worse outcome would be if other countries, acting in their self-interests without U.S. leadership, make the same mistake. This could lead to a zero-sum world in which no country invests in the long-term basic research for the future, while all scramble to compete over the diminishing returns from past investments.

A negative outcome like this is still avoidable. It is the main thrust of this report to show how a loss of global competitiveness can be avoided by increasing the efficiency of U.S. researchers and by positioning the Nation's great research universities and National Laboratories as central engines of innovation and geographical anchors of the U.S. science and technology enterprise.

The farsighted policies outlined in Vannevar Bush's 1945 report, "Science—the Endless Frontier," have served the Nation well.[34] Bush outlined three basic principles: (1) the Government must be the principal source of funding for basic science; (2) basic science should be located primarily in universities that combine research with the education of the next generation of scientists and engineers; and (3) the Government should allocate funding across broad categories of science, but the decisions to allocate funds to particular projects should be made by independent scientific experts (by a process called "peer review"). Although the arguments for these principles are not couched in the language of economics, the first two are sensible responses to market failure. Government should fund basic research because the incomplete appropriability of the results will lead the private sector to invest too little. And the co-location of research with education gives rise to large, positive synergies, ensuring that graduates carry with them into industry knowledge of cutting-edge research, techniques, and instrumentation.

2.3. Transformational Benefits from Research Are Rare, but World-Changing

By its very nature, scientific research is an exploration of the unknown. It is thus not possible to assign to any particular line of research—especially in its basic and early applied stages—an actuarial value or an expected return on investment. This uncertainty diminishes, of course, for parts of the enterprise that move toward more applied research and into development. At that end of the spectrum industry requires, and generally achieves, calculable returns. But this more predictable applied research is fueled by the results of earlier, unpredictable basic research. The policy and economic quandary is thus how to strike the right balance between investment in activities whose return on investment is unpredictable and investment in activities whose return is (at least somewhat) predictable, but depends on the output of the unpredictable pre-cursors.

If returns from basic research are unpredictable, does this mean that they are, on average, small or large? Historical evidence strongly indicates that they are large. It is true that many individual investments in basic research do not produce an identifiable immediate return, even as they fill gaps in scientific understanding. Infrequently, however, but nevertheless with regularity, the return from a particular line of basic research is so large as to be world-changing. The history of scientific and technological advances in the last five centuries, and particularly the last two centuries, reveals a huge spread in the importance and magnitude of discoveries and the benefits flowing from them. Some important discoveries, such as the infection-fighting power of penicillin or a radically different battery technology, are of a magnitude that might occur once in several decades. Others, such as the overlapping revelations that unpredictably led to today's microelectronics and computer industries—the harnessing of electricity, the understanding of atomic structure, and the discovery of quantum mechanics – are of a magnitude that may occur only once in several centuries; it is no exaggeration to call these world-changing.

Basic Research Creates Platforms for New Industries

The most important scientific discoveries are often potentiated by a long period of evolutionary advances whose ultimate significance may not be evident.

Then, at times that are not easily predicted beforehand, evolutionary advances become enabling of single great discoveries – or more often avalanches of related discoveries – that can suddenly be recognized as world-changing. Such cascades, when they occur, reveal new vistas, territories, and platforms on which unanticipated industries can be built.[35]

Start-up companies in these new industries may be risky, in the sense of requiring venture capital that is not risk-averse.

But once the new, common platform exists, competition grows among firms built on that platform, and risks are averaged by diversification. In other words, investments in unpredictable basic research paradoxically produce platforms on which traditional capitalism, with the possibility of predictable returns and investment at acceptable risk, may take over and flourish.

A world in which such platforms are regularly created is a world whose aggregate wealth can rise from one avalanche to the next.

The Rationale for Investment in Unpredictable Opportunities

What is a rational policy for the allocation of resources to unpredictable investments, such as basic research? There is no simple economic answer, because the biggest positive returns are both the least predictable, and also the rarest.

A large fraction of incremental investments on the margin may be expended without any return. The rational strategy requires a patient investor who is able to make steady investments that are not funded out of short-term returns, but rather from a continuing income account.

In the United States, only one such patient investor is evident: the Federal Government. And there is only one ultimate source of funds: the U.S. taxpayer.

These considerations tell us nothing about how generously the rational, patient investor with continuing revenues should fund a long-term investment – yet that is the key question.

What is the right amount for the Federal Government to spend annually on basic and early applied research? Mathematically, if the investor's patience were unlimited and his time horizon infinite, no other investment would be better.[36]

The American people are not infinitely patient; however, they want their children and grandchildren to have better lives than they themselves have had. Probably, they care less about the welfare of people 10 generations from now, ironically, despite their continuing to reap the economic benefits of the industrial revolution 10 generations in the past.

Public Support for Science

PCAST thinks that the American people's willingness to invest in basic and early applied research can be gauged in two ways. The first is the documented "wisdom of crowds"—the public's often tacit understanding that investments in science and technology do pay off economically.[37] This view is not only consistent with scholarly economic research, but is also supported by its own internal logic and consistency.

That is, while the returns from basic research are notoriously difficult to measure within the scope of any finite study, the public's view integrates millions of individual experiences and multigenerational family histories with individual judgments about their value. "How much value do I ascribe to my iPod or Facebook? How valuable is it to me that my grandmother, as a child, was saved by a new drug, so that my mother might be born and I in turn might exist?"

Box 2-1. The Post Office Murals

Recent economic times in the United States have been compared with the tough times of the 1930s. Then, as now, jobs—especially good jobs—were scarce. After a decade of boom years, consumer spending had dropped and industry was operating far below full capacity. Then, as now, people looked to technology to create a future with new industries, new and better jobs, and a better world for their children.

Though fading in history, the tough times and popular aspirations of the Depression remain vibrant and visible today in the many pieces of public art that were created during the 1930s.

More than a thousand murals were commissioned by the Section of Fine Arts of the U.S. Treasury to decorate post offices nationwide.[a] Often mistaken for products of the Works Progress Administration (WPA), these murals were created not primarily to employ artists, but to raise people's spirits with visions of a (it was supposed) heroic past and (it was hoped) prosperous economic future.

While the superficial parallels between then and today are evident, the Post Office murals also provide a metaphor for the deep connections between people's working lives and the highly connected science and technology enterprise that underlies and ultimately creates their jobs. The images on the murals capture the dramatic endpoints of the science and technology enterprise, but to do so, the images have been painted *on* something—a prepared canvas created by basic and early applied research.

Imagine a Post Office mural showing today's technologies. Beneath the picture of a web browser is research at CERN (the European particle physics laboratory) on how to index and share what were then considered to be large quantities of basic physics data. Beneath individualized cancer treatments are not just modern molecular biology and the Human Genome Project, but also the basic and applied research in microelectronics and nanofabrication that enables high-throughput DNA sequencing. Beneath modern manufacturing processes lie basic and applied research in materials, nanosciences, computer modeling (and computers, electronics, and so on), as well as recent advances in statistics. Beneath modern secure web commerce lies the arcane mathematics of number theory.

References:
[a] Patricia Raynor, "Off the Wall: New Deal Post Office Murals," En Route (Oct.-Dec., 1997). www.postalmuseum.si.edu/resources

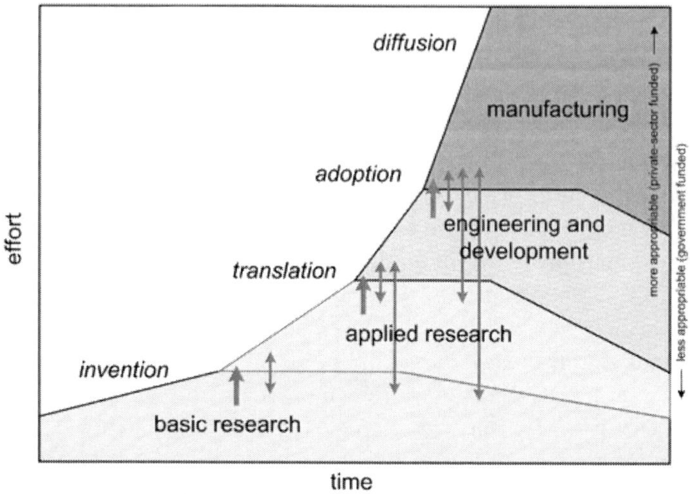

Note: For any one particular product, each stage of technology development acts as a continuing platform for the development of the next. Basic research creates new opportunities for applied research. Engineering development and even manufacturing frequently can directly exploit the results of new basic research, which also feed the inspirations for new research directions back into basic and applied research. In fact, within any technology, all the technology development stages continue to interact with one another during its entire lifetime.

Figure 2-1. Interacting Technology Stages.

The second gauge, discussed previously in Section 2.1, is the American public's strong appetite for noneconomic benefits of science and belief that science and invention are inseparable from America's sense of itself and of its place in the world (see Box 2.1). Not only does science lead to jobs; it leads to better jobs, performed by a better educated population, in a nation that, we hope, will continue to lead the world in prosperity and in democratic social values. As long as these views are widely held by us, the American public, we are justified as patient investors in maintaining, or even extending, both our time horizon and the amount we are willing to invest. In 2010, 82 percent of Americans expressed support for government funding of basic research.[38]

The Value of the Potentiating Evolutionary Research

While the largest benefits of scientific research may come from rare, world-changing avalanches of discovery, those events are potentiated by the steady support of evolutionary scientific advance. That is, great discoveries depend on the actions of many people framing many hypotheses and trying many approaches. Moreover, for any given product or invention that is brought to the marketplace, each stage of technology development acts as a continuing platform for the development of the next, as well as enriching and inspiring new discoveries in the earlier developmental stages (see Figure 2-1). This is a picture very different from a linear model in which the flow of knowledge from basic research to applied research is unidirectional. Retrospectively, we rightly celebrate the discoveries and inventions that change the world, but these changes will not occur without a continuing bidirectional flow of patient and incremental actions by talented researchers. The steady and consistent financial support for these people and institutions underlies the continuing generation of unexpectedly important research outcomes. In a well-balanced system, such steady support coexists with mechanisms for supporting the high-risk, high-return work that may signify the start of a world-changing cascade.

III. A Global Reorganization of Research Is Happening

Increased competition in the private sector, including international competition, drives structural changes in national economies. If the competitive playing field is level, these changes create greater global economic efficiency and, at least in the short run, greater overall wealth. However, they also have consequences that can affect the trajectories of nations in ways other than economic.

The U.S. research enterprise is not immune from these global changes – quite the contrary. The United States is in the midst of a profound reorganization of how research is done, who does it, and how its results find their way to the marketplace. Since this reorganization is happening incrementally, as an evolutionary response to a changing world, it is easy to overlook its breadth and depth and its far-reaching consequences. We made the case in Chapter 2 that for Americans, scientific discovery is not just an economic activity, it is also a core national value and a key part of how they see themselves in the world. As the Nation's policies work to give private-sector industry unfettered access to world markets, they must also work to ensure that U.S. industry will have timely and unfettered access to the abundant flow of inventions and discoveries that have always fueled its competitiveness. It is not automatic that this will happen. The Nation needs proactive policies, along with strengthening changes in its educational and research institutions.

This chapter describes the forces that are driving the global reorganization of research and the responses of U.S. institutions, especially research universities. It is a time of change and ferment, and therefore of opportunity. To seize that opportunity, the United States must act systematically and strategically.

3.1. U.S. Intellectual Capital: Universities, National Laboratories, Industry

In a time of challenge, the United States needs to understand the strengths and assets that it brings to the challenge. The Nation must also make a clear-eyed assessment of its comparative advantages with respect to the rest of the world. Where does the United States lead the world, and where is it falling behind? Only then can a decision be made about how to move forward. The United States retains a strong position in almost all areas of science and technology, and is the undoubted world leader in many areas; but, complacency is not an acceptable strategy.

The three pillars of the U.S. research enterprise are its research universities, its National Laboratories, and American industry's substantial commitment to basic and applied research. The role of these three elements in U.S. and global innovation has evolved greatly over the last 150 years and is in the midst of an additional evolution today. To formulate a strategy for the future, we first need to understand where we are today.

World's Leading Universities

The United States has the world's greatest research universities. In the 2011–2012 London Times Higher Education World University Rankings, the United States leads with 75 of the world's top 200 research universities, followed by the United Kingdom (32) and Germany (12). At the very top, 7 of the top 10 institutions and 18 of the top 25 institutions are in the United States.[39] The 2011 Academic Ranking of World Universities (ARWU) gives a similar view. A total of 151 U.S. institutions are in the top 500 universities worldwide (second is the UK with 37), with eight U.S. universities in the top 10 and 17 in the top 20 (no change from the previous year).[40]

These rankings recognize important indicators of scientific leadership and expertise, including the number of Nobel Prizes and Fields Medals[41] awarded; the number of articles published in leading journals and periodicals; citations in other publications; and performance in proportion to an institution's size (so that smaller institutions are not disadvantaged).

Researchers in the United States lead the world both in the volume of articles published and in the frequency with which those papers are cited by others. U.S.-based authors contributed to one-third of all scientific articles worldwide in 2001.[42] These publication data are significant because they reflect original research productivity and because the professional reputations, job prospects, and career advancement of researchers depend on their ability to publish significant findings in open, peer-reviewed literature.

As noted by the Augustine panel, the United States also excels in higher education and training for research.[43] A recent comparison concluded that 38 of the world's 50 leading research institutions are in the United States.[44] These are the institutions that draw the interest of the world's best young scientists. For decades, the United States has been the destination of choice for science and engineering graduate students and for postdoctoral scholars choosing to study outside their home countries, but that trend is now moving in the opposite direction. Of all students who studied abroad in 2000, 23 percent chose to study in the United States. By 2009, this had declined to 18 percent.[45]

World's leading National Laboratories

The United States is also unique in the world in the range and quality of its Federal and National Laboratories.[46] It has world-leading laboratories in biomedical research, energy, and space exploration that span the spectrum from basic research to applied research for specific national needs. Individual National Laboratories, most with a special legal status as Federally Funded Research and Development Centers (FFRDCs), are sponsored by several agencies, notably including the Department of Energy (DOE) (with both science laboratories and national security laboratories), the National Science Foundation, NASA, and the Department of Defense.

Most Federal laboratories, including those run by the National Institutes of Health (NIH), the National Aeronautics and Space Administration (NASA), the Department of Agriculture (USDA), and the Environmental Protection Agency (EPA), are Government-Owned, Government-Operated (GOGO). Conversely, all but one of the DOE National Laboratories are Government-Owned, Contractor-Operated (GOCO), as is NASA's Jet Propulsion Laboratory (JPL). GOGO and GOCO laboratories operate under quite different legislative authorities, the distinction being particularly important regarding technology transfer.

The importance of FFRDCs shows up in many of the Nation's greatest scientific accomplishments. JPL, for example, has a history reaching back to before World War II. Scientists at JPL, originally the Guggenheim Aerospace Laboratory of the California Institute of Technology (Caltech), had been working with the U.S. Army on a series of rockets when, on October 4, 1957, the Soviet Union stunned the world with the launch of Sputnik, the first satellite to orbit Earth. An immediate response was imperative. The government turned to the U.S. Army's Ballistic Missile Agency in Huntsville, Alabama, and to JPL. Their efforts culminated on January 31, 1958, with the launch of the first U.S. satellite, Explorer 1, which sent back data about the radiation environment high above Earth's surface. Thus began the "space race" with the Soviet Union. When President Eisenhower created the National Aeronautics and Space Administration later in 1958, he transferred JPL into the new agency, keeping it under Caltech management.[47] Another example is the Manhattan Project to develop the first nuclear weapons, in which research was conducted at the Los Alamos National Laboratory in New Mexico but was managed by the University of California under a government contract.

The Federal Acquisition Regulations that govern FFRDCs note that their long-term relationships with the government provide continuity to attract talented people to work on national needs with objectivity and independence. The FFRDCs are familiar with the needs of the sponsoring agency and are able to provide a quick-response capability.[48]

U.S. Industry

From the Yankee watchmaker, through Henry Ford's manufacturing revolution, Bell Laboratories, Xerox PARC, and today's research-intensive corporations, the United States has benefited from the innovative spirit of its industry—a spirit that has impelled Americans to discover and invent things, not just produce them. In 2009, 48 percent of all applied research in the United States was funded by industry, as was 78 percent of development. Industry-funded R&D, especially development, thus dominates the technological ecosystem.[49] The R&D accomplishments of private firms, and their effective and robust partnerships with universities, other private-sector companies, and the Federal Government, have been major factors in the past success of the U.S. research enterprise, yielding benefits vital to many sectors of industry.

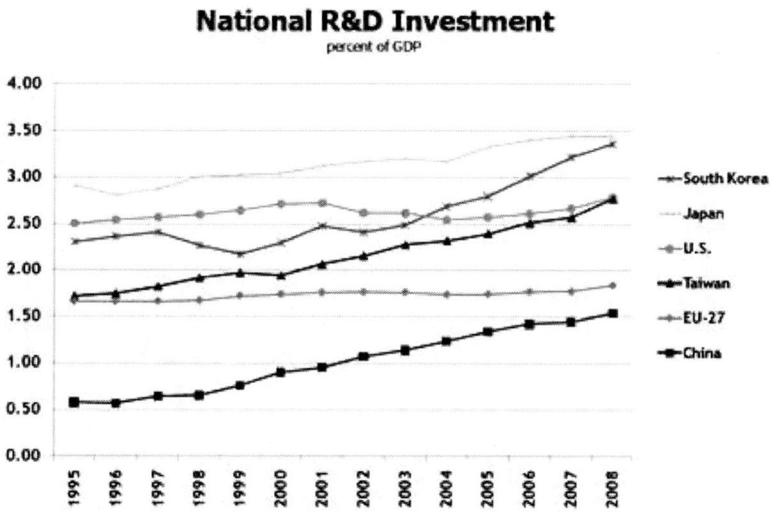

Source: Patrick J. Clemens, "Historical Trends in Federal R&D," AAAS. Data source: OECD, Main Science and Technology Indicators, February 2011.

Figure 3-1. National R&D Investment.

In contrast to the continuing preeminence of U.S. universities, however, the intensity of U.S. industrial R&D investment has not kept up with the rest of the world. As a fraction of GDP, U.S. R&D investment now ties for eighth in the world, behind countries such as Korea, Japan, Switzerland, and Israel (Figure 3-1). U.S. R&D investments increasingly lag other countries as a percentage of their respective GDPs. South Korea has overtaken the United States and continues to grow, while China and Taiwan show long-term continuous growth relative to the roughly flat U.S. investment.

Although total U.S. R&D is still greater than that of any other single country, from 1999 to 2009, the U.S. share of the world's R&D investment shrank from 38 percent to 31 percent.[50] China is now the world's second-largest R&D performer. In 2008, its universities produced more Ph.D.'s (49,698 across all fields) than the United States.[51] Countries in Asia collectively performed 32 percent of world R&D in 2009, edging out the U.S. total.[52] Singapore's government drives its flagship research universities (The National University of Singapore, Nanyang Technological University, and Singapore Management University[53]) to assess their quality against international peers, with considerable and continuing success.[54] More published scientific papers come from the European Union (about 250,000 in 2007) than from the United States.[55] While the United States still retains leadership in most areas of research and development investment and success, these are trends of enormous significance. As we will see in the next two sections, they drive the need to strengthen and expand relationships between U.S. industry and American universities and National Laboratories.

3.2. Research in Industry Has Shifted Dramatically

Industry dominates the total U.S. investment in R&D, with about two-thirds of R&D performed by private firms. As a 60-year trend, industry's share of R&D funding, relative to that of the Federal Government, has risen almost continuously (Figure 3-2).

However, the nature of industry R&D has evolved dramatically over the past two decades in ways that may be putting basic research, the seed corn of the entire S&T enterprise, at risk. Put simply, as the larger fraction of R&D has shifted to industry, its time horizon has correspondingly gotten shorter.

The Classic Corporate Research Labs Are Gone

Historically, the innovation capability of the United States included a number of informal public-private partnerships, with legendary centers such as Bell Labs, RCA Labs, Xerox Palo Alto Research Center (PARC), and others playing a notable role.

Each of these privately run organizations supported side by side basic research and research with clear commercial potential. The commercialization of new products arising from these research efforts relied on a mix of corporate funding and venture capital.[56]

Since the 1990s, however, research at corporate laboratories of this type has shifted from open-ended problem-solving to short-term commercial exploitation.

The great industrial centers of basic research, such as Bell Labs and RCA Labs, flourished in times very different from now. Regulated monopolies, or stable consumer-brand preferences, gave these companies strong, predictable cash flows. They were able to take risks, despite the uncertainty of translating basic research into new products. However, since the 1990s, the industrial landscape has changed.

Predictable cash flows and regulated monopolies are largely things of the past, meaning that companies today are far less able to conduct research with a long-term view.[57]

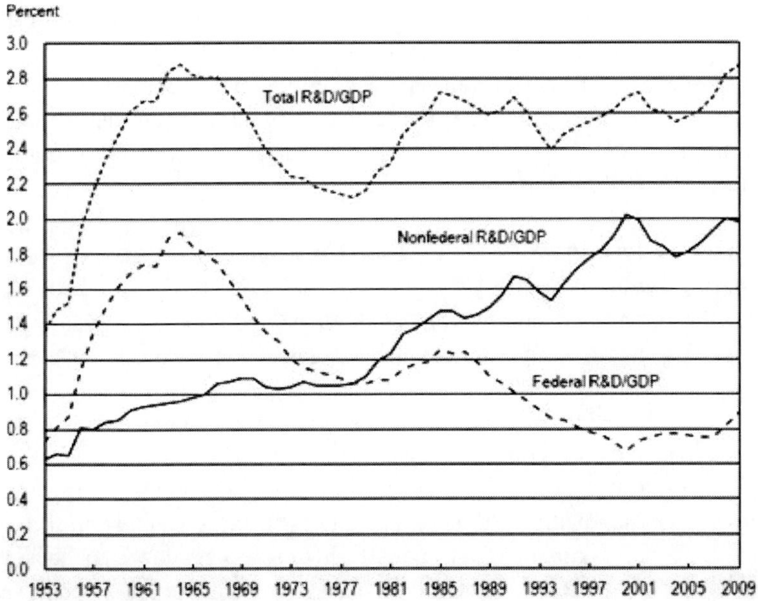

GDP = gross domestic product.

Notes: Some figures involve estimates and may later be revised. Federal R&D/GDP ratios represent federal government as a funder of R&D by all performers; nonfederal ratios reflect all other sources of R&D funding.

Source: National Science Foundation, National Center for Science and Engineering Statistics, National Patterns of R&D Resources.

Note: Since the 1960s, total expenditures on R&D have grown with the U.S. economy, so that its ratio to GDP has not dramatically changed. However, the Federal share has decreased significantly, with the balance taken up by industry.

Figure 3-2. Ratio of U.S. R&D to Gross Domestic Product, Roles of Federal and Non-Federal Funding for R&D: 1953-2009.

Bell Labs offers a clear example of this evolution. Originally founded in 1925 by AT&T and Western Electric (AT&T's manufacturing arm), its mission was to produce practical innovations for the subsidiary Bell System telephone companies. It went on to produce six Nobel Prizes in physics, including one for inventing the transistor. Starting in 2001, however, Bell Labs suffered a series of drastic cuts to its funding and staff. In 2001, Bell Labs had 30,000 employees; now owned by Alcatel-Lucent, it has just 1,000. Similarly, RCA Labs produced a string of break-throughs in the 1950s and 1960s, including color TV, lasers, solar cells, and infrared imaging. Now part of

Sarnoff Corporation, it has a significantly reduced budget and focuses only on developing smaller technologies with a commercial focus.[58]

The decline of these and other pioneering research laboratories (see Box 3-1) has significantly cut into the foundation of basic research that the United States needs to fuel industrial innovation. Universities and Federal laboratories are increasingly filling this gap.

Increased Competition Leads to Underinvestment in Basic and Early Applied Research

In the global economy, companies that traditionally capitalized on regional U.S. markets must now compete against organizations all over the world. The speed with which products and services can be delivered around the world, from and to almost anywhere, diminishes the home-field advantage that used to shield local companies against foreign competitors.

As a result, corporations with an obligation to shareholders now tend to underinvest in innovation, because no single business can capture all the economic benefits arising from new technologies, products, or business models (see Section 2.2).[59] Private firms are far more concerned about R&D investments that will give them an immediate competitive advantage and therefore choose to invest only in low-risk endeavors, which are often closer to the development and implementation end of the spectrum.[60]

This increased competition has reduced industry's ability to support basic research. Since the focus on shareholder value began in the early 1990s, industry's support of basic research, that is, research with more than a 3-to 5-year time horizon, has remained roughly flat in constant dollars (Figure 3-3). In the same period up to 2008, overall basic research expenditures approximately doubled, largely indicative of a shift to Federal responsibility for support of basic research. Since 1953, the fraction of industry R&D spent on basic research has fluctuated on decadal time scales, with a historic high of 7.9 percent and low of 4.2 percent. In 2009, about 5 percent of total industry R&D funding went to basic research, 15 percent went to applied research, and the rest went to development.[61] IBM, Microsoft, and Hewlett-Packard collectively spend $17 billion per year on R&D, but only 3–5 percent of that goes to basic science.[62] Many also argue that current support levels for basic research may be overstated because of drifts in the definition of what is called "basic," a trend noted in Department of Defense-supported research and more generally by many members of PCAST.[63]

Box 3-1. The Changing Structure of Corporate Research: PARC in Two Eras

Then

In 1970, Xerox Corporation recruited a world-class team of experts in information and physical sciences to form the heart of its new Palo Alto Research Center (PARC). PARC's mission was to create "The Office of the Future." Over the following 40 years, it pioneered a series of widely influential technologies: laser printing, object-oriented programming, Ethernet and distributed computing, the graphical-user interface, and optical storage. In the early years, XEROX funded PARC as a corporate laboratory and licensed technology to others. In this way, innovations from PARC fueled the rise of companies such as Apple, 3COM, and Adobe.

Now

In 2002, Xerox converted PARC from a corporate laboratory to a wholly owned but independent subsidiary. With its state-of-the-art laboratories and leading scientists, PARC continues research in the physical, computer, and social sciences to develop breakthroughs for its partners and clients. PARC is active in core areas like cleantech and energy, intelligent automation, flow cytometry, LEDs and laser diodes, and image recognition. It functions as an outsourced research center, and currently has about 25 large corporate clients and government agencies that fund individual research projects up front and own the rights to the resulting work. Clients include Samsung (networking technology), Dentsu (demographics), Sun Microsystems (interconnects for high-speed servers), Dowa (ultraviolet light-emitting devices), NEC (human interfaces), Motorola (conversation analysis), and Fujitsu (ubiquitous computing). PARC also conducts research not funded by partners, in projects of interest to its staff. The results of these projects are owned by XEROX, which also benefits from a valuable halo effect in high-tech industry. Start-ups have also been spun out of PARC. One of the best known is Powerset, which pioneered natural-language search and was acquired by Microsoft in 2008. Today, PARC has a staff of about 200 people.

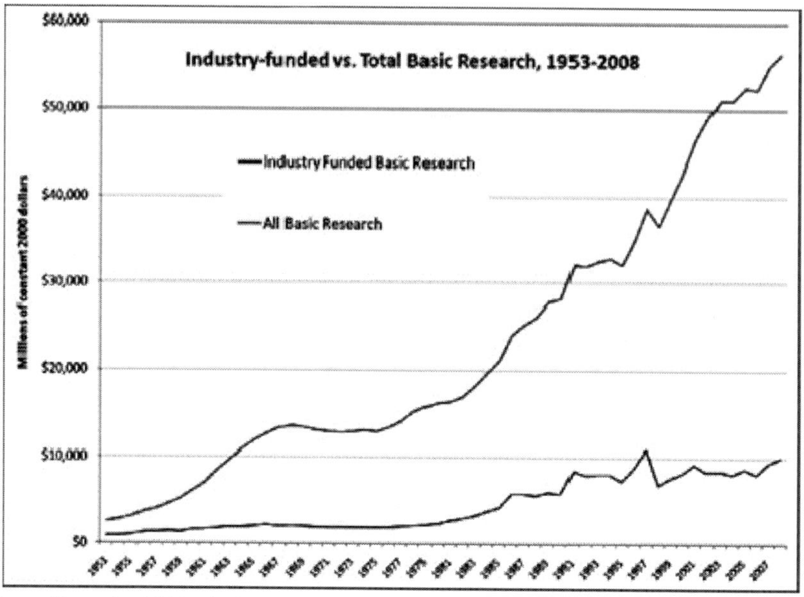

Note: Since the 1990s, industry funding of basic research has remained relatively flat, while total basic research, largely Federally supported, has continued to grow with the U.S. GDP. Data source: NSF, "National Patterns of R&D Resources: 2008 Data Update"

Figure 3-3. Industry Funded and Total Basic Research, 1953–2008.

Globalization Leads to Migration of R&D Offshore

Globalization allows U.S. corporations to perform many aspects of R&D more cost effectively offshore. Not only is the cost of skilled workers often lower, but the availability of such workers, such as trained scientists and engineers is perceived to be higher. The inadequate number of U.S. college graduates with STEM degrees is a large contributing factor to this perception.[64] Moving R&D offshore is a rational economic choice for the companies themselves, but it has negative long-term consequences for the United States. A recent survey by Ernst & Young found that 11 percent of companies based in North America are now spending more than a quarter of their R&D budgets in countries with emerging markets, such as India and China. Moreover, 23 percent of companies expect to be doing so within 5 years.[65]

To give just one example, a major U.S. chemical company has in the past 5 years established R&D laboratories in China, India, and Brazil. These countries did not provide direct subsidies, although India streamlined the permitting process for building the facility. In China and India, the U.S. company is partnering with several major institutes and universities. The number of employees in these three laboratories is about 12 percent of the total employed in its U.S. science and technology operations. The company already has R&D facilities in Taiwan, Japan, Germany, and Switzerland.[66]

Of course, globalization also allows foreign companies to move research activities to the United States, and many are doing so. For example, foreign-owned multinational corporations (MNCs) actually do somewhat more research in the United States than U.S.-owned multinational corporations do abroad.[67] Such net flows are advantageous to the United States, but even if the net flow were zero, the flows themselves would not be without consequences. The appropriability of returns from research to the U.S. economy (see Section 2.2) is likely highest when the research is both generated and used within the United States. When either side of the research transaction is abroad (i.e., for both directions of flow), it seems likely that the benefit to the United States is lessened in the long run. The ability to harness such facilities for U.S. needs during an international crisis (Section 2.1) might also be compromised.

Consequences of These Changes

The United States today has fewer and smaller corporate laboratories than it did just a generation ago. Research by industry now focuses more on development and less on basic and applied research; true basic research (fundamental research done with no specific application in mind) has especially diminished. Since industry investment in R&D is twice as much as that by the Federal Government, this shift has had a particularly devastating effect on industry-supported *basic* research. Furthermore, as R&D increasingly migrates offshore, it is becoming clear that innovation is likely to migrate with it.

One study found that private industry is developing fewer of the most important innovations than it did almost 40 years ago.[68] The majority of these award-winning innovations now arise instead from early discoveries supported through Federal funding and university-based research. Universities and National Laboratories are among the few places that still engage in the type of game-changing and disruptive research that has led to many of the most significant U.S. technological advancements. In 2008, 64 percent of the research papers cited in patent applications were written by university faculty, up from 58 percent just one decade earlier.[69]

PCAST's report on advanced manufacturing documents a loss of U.S. leadership in manufacturing industries based on inventions and knowledge originating in the United States.[70] As manufacturing leadership erodes, R&D activity, as illustrated by the previous anecdote of the chemical company, is moving offshore to gain access to global markets and to respond to global competition for technical talent and the increasing supply of skilled scientists and engineers abroad. While U.S. leadership in manufacturing is declining, other nations are investing heavily in R&D. An accounting by Battelle projects that over 2 years, between 2010 and 2012, the United States' share of global R&D will drop from 32.8 percent to 31.1 percent, while Asian countries, already outspending the United States in aggregate, will increase their combined share from 34.3 percent to 36.7 percent.[71]

3.3. American Universities Are Adopting Additional Roles

American universities have always changed with the times to meet national needs, and they continue to do so today. As generators of ground-breaking research, U.S. universities still lead the world, but stagnating industry expenditures on basic and early applied research and the rapid pace of change in the global economy are propelling the research universities into a new era. They are additionally becoming the new centers of the engine of innovation, the basic and applied research arms for much of U.S. high-tech industry.

In a historical context, we can see this transformation as the third major "augmentation" of the U.S. university. To understand how change can come to universities, it is useful to review what we consider the two previous augmentations and their significance for the Nation's growth.

First Augmentation: The Morrill Act (1862)

Before the Civil War, U.S. universities were mainly located on the east coast, emphasized classical studies, and served only a small fraction of the population. In 1862, as the country's west-ward expansion gathered pace, Justin Smith Morrill, a Congressman (later Senator) from Vermont, felt that the American people needed practical education on a large scale to give them the skills to tackle the real-world problems they faced. Morrill's advocacy led Congress to pass two laws that altered the fundamental focus of U.S. universities, the Morrill Act of 1862[72] and the Morrill Act of 1890.[73]

The first of these created the nationwide system of land grant colleges that continues to the present day. In 1862, the areas of great national need were agriculture, mechanical arts, and home economics. Land grant colleges were created to provide, in each State of the Union, education in these crucial areas. Beyond education, furthermore, faculty members were expected to conduct research in these areas and share the results of this research with the surrounding communities through outreach programs.[74]

The Morrill Act of 1862 also gave the Federal Government a direct role in supporting higher education. The Act granted each state 30,000 acres of public land for each of its congressional delegation members. States used proceeds from the sale of this land to create trusts dedicated to the support of teaching and research. Many large public universities owe their origin to this farsighted act, which was also important to the history of Cornell University and the Massachusetts Institute of Technology (MIT).

In the post-Civil War era, the Morrill Act of 1890 required states to ensure equal-opportunity admissions to its Land Grant colleges or else create separate institutions for people of color. Many of today's historically black colleges and universities (HBCUs) were founded in response. However, the main thrust of the 1890 Act was to increase the funding of the land grant colleges "to promote the liberal and practical education of the industrial classes."

These laws changed the course of higher education and shaped the focus of colleges and universities for almost 100 years.

Second Augmentation: The Post-World War II Vannevar Bush Era

Until World War II, the Federal Government's support of universities continued to emphasize the teaching of practical skills. Acting independently, a few universities had established research laboratories, shifting to a focus on fundamental knowledge and inquiry. An early example was Harvard University's Jefferson Physical Laboratory, created in 1870. By World War II, several U.S. universities had established themselves as top-tier research institutions, despite the lack of direct support from the Federal Government.[75]

The fundamental purpose of Federal Government support for universities changed dramatically following the release of a report, "Science—the Endless Frontier," requested by and submitted to President Harry Truman in July 1945 by Vannevar Bush, formerly Dean of Engineering at MIT and then President of the Carnegie Institution of Washington. The report argued that it was in the nation's best interest for the Federal Government to fund university research: "The Federal Government should accept new responsibilities for promoting the creation of new scientific knowledge and the development of scientific talent in our youth."[76]

The report emphasized not only the obligation of the government to support basic research, but also the unique role universities play in this endeavor:

> The publicly and privately supported colleges, universities, and research institutes are the centers of basic research. They are the wellsprings of knowledge and understanding. As long as they are vigorous and healthy and their scientists are free to pursue the truth wherever it may lead, there will be a flow of new scientific knowledge to those who can apply it to practical problems in Government, in industry, or elsewhere.[77]

The next 50 years witnessed a dramatic rise in Federal support for basic research. It created and drove the university research enterprise. The Federal Government went on to create the National Science Foundation in 1950 and greatly boost funding for the National Institutes of Health.[78] Facing the challenge of the new space age with the launch of Sputnik in 1957, the Federal Government was able to use this infrastructure, further enabled by the National Defense Education Act, to enlarge the cohort of students in STEM fields at all levels. The institutions created in the 1950s, along with the newer DOE, remain today the primary stewards of basic research. The partnership between universities and Federal agencies, in support of both research and education, led to some of the most profound and world-changing discoveries of the 20th century.

Thus, two generations ago, the United States got it right in "connecting the dots" from basic research in science and technology to national prosperity. We now recognize that the benefits from research result not just from a linear progression, where basic research in an area leads to applied research, development, and products in that same area. Rather, basic research fuels a whole innovation ecosystem, often in unpredictable ways.

Today, we must learn from the success of the two previous augmentations of the U.S. research universities and take actions that position the United States for continued leadership in the world in science and technology. This means that the United States needs to protect its ability to generate foundational basic research while also doing more to enable the fruits of that research to become platforms for products, jobs, and new industries. The underlying question, the creative tension that this report seeks to address, is: What set of policies best propel these two goals simultaneously?

Today's Third Augmentation: Central Hubs of the Innovation Ecosystem

With the proportionate decline of investment in basic and early applied research by industry and specialized research laboratories, U.S. research universities are today performing not only the basic research for which they have been best known during the last 50 years, but also to an increasing extent applied and translational research with the potential to deliver innovations, new industries, and market efficiencies over the next 50 years. Today, U.S. research universities are closer to the marketplace than they have ever been, with a new focus on translating and transferring research discoveries to industry.

Research universities are increasingly passing their results to the private sector. The 1980 Bayh-Dole Act gave universities patent and intellectual property rights over the results of research funded by the Federal Government; previously, those rights belonged to the Government. In the next section, we detail how Bayh-Dole has transformed the relationship between universities and industry.

Universities, along with the National Laboratories, are also increasingly hubs of research for needs such as national security, health, and environmental stewardship. In earlier decades domestic corporate laboratories such as Bell Labs could be tapped by Government as needs arose. That era is past.

As industry works with universities as a key source of innovation, the type of research industry is funding has evolved. While funding some basic research, industry increasingly funds applied projects to solve specific technical issues. Companies may also collaborate with other corporations in the same or different fields, but it is to academia that they increasingly turn for:

- Exposure to leading-edge thinking and technology, and insight from internationally recognized experts.
- Objective advice on strategic decision-making, related to new products and to implementing innovative management practices.
- Research partnerships.
- Recruitment of skilled employees with fresh perspectives and state-of-the-art knowledge who can become future company leaders.

The last point deserves some amplification. Large technology companies are increasingly developing partnerships with research universities with the primary purpose of attracting top young engineers and scientists to their field, even if not always to their company. As one educator describes it, "What large companies want is a relationship that involves student transfer as much as anything else. They want interns to come in as undergraduate and graduate students. They want access to them as new hires."[79] Dow Chemical recently committed $250 million to chemical engineering departments over the next 10 years, with the explicit purpose of expanding the pool of Ph.D.'s. "Excellence in scientific education and the development of innovative solutions go hand-in-hand," said Andrew N. Liveris, Dow's Chairman and Chief Executive Officer about this initiative. "We are pleased to partner with academia to ensure that a vital pipeline of talent and research is available to fuel the discoveries and solutions of tomorrow."[80]

George Brown (D-Calif.), whom many scientists consider one of the most visionary members of Congress of the last 50 years, was the long-time chairman of the House Committee on Science, Space and Technology and (after 1994) ranking minority member of the House Science Committee. He was one of the chief sponsors of the legislation that created the White House Office of Science and Technology Policy in 1976. A few years before his death in 1999, he reviewed decades of his past speeches and concluded, "I am struck by how often I have pleaded with the scientific community to pay attention to the changes taking place in the world and the need to become more closely linked with social goals and needs."[81] While Congressman Brown might be pleased at the significant steps that American universities have taken in the last 10 years, much remains to be done. That is the thrust of much of the rest of this report.

Example of the New Role: Proof-of-Concept Centers

Embracing their new role, a number of research universities have established proof-of-concept centers that provide seed funding for early-stage research that would not be funded by any conventional source. These centers fill the gap between pure university research and angel investment or venture capital support for start-ups. They differ from "incubators" in two important ways. First, research in incubators is often fenced off from university activities, whereas proof-of-concept centers allow the faculty and students they fund to perform research in their university laboratories. Second, incubators typically offer seed money or a shared office environment to businesses that already have a product, whereas proof-of-concept centers aim to explore the commercial viability of potential products springing from research.

Proof-of-concept centers as realized thus far include some or all of the following features:

- They facilitate interaction between university innovators and industry; they include advisory mentors and industry catalysts.
- They provide seed funding for commercialization of promising research; they assist with market evaluation and business plan development.
- They support educational programs to prepare students and researchers for entrepreneurship.
- They hold special events to showcase technologies and entrepreneurs and promote the exchange of ideas and formation of new collaborations.

Proof-of-concept centers provide venture capitalists and angel investors an easier entre to possible start-ups at the pre-incorporation phase. They are generally separated from the university technology-transfer office to avoid conflicts in acting as advocates for the faculty or student innovator. Box 3-2 highlights MIT's Deshpande Center, an example of a proof-of-concept center. Another early pioneer has been the von Liebig Center at the University of California at San Diego's Jacobs School of Engineering.[82]

Over the past 10 years, the success of these two centers has inspired others. Similar entrepreneurial initiatives exist at the University of Utah, the Georgia Institute of Technology (Georgia Tech), the University of Kansas, Boston University, the University of Vermont, and the University of Southern California. The University of Utah created the Technology Commercialization Office, which by now has now helped arrange the networking and funding resources for 25 companies.[83]

We will have more to say about proof-of-concept centers, and why they are important, in Section 4.1.

3.4. Enhanced Partnerships Are Growing

As the character of industry research has changed, as universities and National Laboratories have been thrust into important new roles, and as the role of Government has consequently evolved, novel kinds of partnerships have come into existence. In this section we review some of them. Many of our recommendations in Chapters 4 and 5 are targeted at increasing the effectiveness of the kinds of partnerships described here.

Box 3-2. MIT's Deshpande Center

The Deshpande Center was established at the MIT School of Engineering in 2002 to increase the impact of MIT technologies in the marketplace. Founded with an initial $20 million donation from entrepreneur Desh Deshpande, the Center has raised further financial support from alumni, entrepreneurs, and investors to provide a sustainable source of funding.

The Deshpande Center supports emerging technologies, including biotechnology, biomedical devices, information technology, new materials, nanotechnology, and energy innovations. It sponsors a grant program, a catalyst (mentor) program, innovation teams (i-Teams), and events. Since its start in 2002, the center has received more than 500 proposals from over 250 faculty members. Its 90 funded projects (totaling $11 million) have supported more than 300 faculty members and their students. The center has engaged more than 100 volunteers from the venture and entrepreneur community and has seen the creation of 26 companies that have raised over $350 million in funding and employ more than 400 people.

Anyone at MIT can submit a three-page pre-proposal. Full proposals (10 pages) are then requested and evaluated through technical peer review and a team presentation. Volunteer catalysts/mentors of outside industry experts are offered to successful teams, along with access to a technology licensing officer.

"Ignition" grants ($25,000–$50,000) are typically awarded for technologies that are 3 or 4 years away from spinning out of the university. They enable MIT faculty members, together with students, post-docs, and staff, to take risks and explore uncharted concepts before they have a developed proof of concept or have gathered any data. "Innovation" grants (up to $250,000) go to projects that are within 1 to 2 years of spin-out.

Source: Information gathered from the Deshpande Center website "Deshpande Center for Technological Innovation," MIT School of Engineering, Massachusetts Institute of Technology, accessed January 31, 2012, web.mit.edu/deshpandecenter.

Partnerships between Universities and Industry

Universities perform about 57 percent of the Nation's basic research but only about 12 percent of applied research. Industry performs only 17 percent of the basic research, 69 percent of the applied research, and virtually all the development.[84] These numbers illustrate how the transformation of a discovery or idea from basic research into a commercial product almost always involves a transition from university to industry.

Historically, many universities have had industrial-liaison programs. These represent one of the earliest university-industry relationships to emerge. The programs typically foster relationships between university faculty members and industrial partners; they can facilitate research and faculty interactions, as well as provide insight into new technologies and management practices. One of the most successful examples is at MIT, whose Industrial Liaison Program was founded in 1948. It has relationships with 190 companies both in the United States and abroad, whose membership fees bring in approximately $9.7 million per year.[85]

Today, industry-university partnerships have become vastly more varied and complex. They include sponsored research agreements, joint research projects, industry memberships in research institutes, licensing of university patents, graduate fellowships, endowed faculty chairs, student internships, and start-up companies that are spun out of academia. Most of these partnerships have developed naturally to serve the mutual interests of the companies and academic researchers. The Federal Government's primary role is not to participate directly in these relationships but to establish the policy environment in which they can flourish, through the Bayh-Dole Act, the Patent Reform Act, parts of the tax code, and other legislation.

The Bayh-Dole Act (1980) has made technology licensing a major partnering activity between universities and industry. The Association of University Technology Managers (AUTM) has documented the steady growth of licensing.[86] From 1991 to 2010, the number of patent applications filed by universities rose from an average of 14 to 67 per institution, with a total of 4,469 patents issued in FY 2010 to the 183 universities, research institutions, and hospitals that responded to AUTM's survey. A total of 4,735 licenses or options were executed in 2010 on the patents owned by the 155 universities in the AUTM survey, 34 percent going to large companies, 49 percent to small companies, and 18 percent to startups. In the same period (1991 to 2010), licensing income increased from $1.9 million to $13 million per institution, for a total of $2.4 billion in Fiscal Year 2010 (FY2010).

Patents are not the only way that technology moves from the campus to the market, however. Hundreds of start-ups are generated each year on the basis of university-developed technology. The AUTM survey records 651 startups based on university-licensed technologies in FY2010 alone (up from 212 in 1994), with about 75 percent of these start-ups located in the same state as the university. The number of start-ups is, over the long run, roughly proportional to the total research activity at each campus, with about one start-up per $100 million of research expenditures. These start-ups are not the principal outcome of most academic research, but they do represent a very important additional benefit. Moreover, according to a report by the Science Coalition, "Companies spun out of research universities have a far greater success rate than other companies, creating good jobs and spurring economic activity."[87]

Universities are also working with industry partners to organize novel institutes designed to integrate the industrial partners more closely into the research on campus. Two of many possible examples are the following:

- The Energy Biosciences Institute (EBI) was established in 2007 as a joint institute of the University of California Berkeley, Lawrence Berkeley National Laboratory, The University of Illinois at Urbana-Champaign, and British Petroleum (BP). BP invested $50 million per year in the Institute over a period of 10 years. The governance board has eight members, four from the university-national laboratory sector and four from BP. The relationship among the partners is defined in a historic master agreement, which is available online.[88]
- The Solid State Lighting and Energy Center (SSLEC) at the University of California, Santa Barbara, which was established in 2007. Fourteen companies from related industries are members of this institute, which does research in high-efficiency LEDs, lasers for displays, transistors for power switching, and wide-bandgap solar cells, all based on compound semiconductors. The total funding provided by the industry partners is $7 million per year. The roadmap for the SSLEC research program is determined through constant interaction between the industry partners and the SSLEC Executive Board. The center is now generating one patent for roughly every $500,000 of funding, and the partnership agreement gives the industry partners first licensing rights.[89]

Some Federal support is commendably targeted at broadening university interactions with the private sector. For example, NSF's Innovation Corps (I-Corps), announced in 2011, creates a new national network of scientists, engineers, innovators, business leaders, and entrepreneurs centered on providing mentoring opportunities that will enhance research transfer.[90]

Partnerships within Industry

The ways in which private sector entities can partner with each other on research activities has diversified over the past two decades. In one of the oldest models, some industries have formed consortia that invest in university research to help solve the technical challenges facing the industry as a whole and to develop technical talent for their member companies. The Semiconductor Industry Association (SIA), founded in 1977 by five microelectronics pioneers, represents 60 companies that account for 80 percent of the Nation's semiconductor production. In 1982, the SIA set up the Semiconductor Research Corporation (SRC), an industry consortium that invests and manages several semiconductor research programs. Since its founding, SRC has managed more than $1.2 billion in research funds and has supported nearly 9,000 students and 2,000 faculty at 257 universities, resulting in more than 50,000 technical documents and 373 patents. In 2007, SRC was awarded the National Medal of Technology for (1) building the world's largest and most successful university research force in support of the rapid growth and 10,000-fold advances of the semiconductor industry, (2) proving the concept of collaborative research as the first high-technology research consortium, and (3) creating the concept and methodology that evolved into the International Technology Roadmap for Semiconductors.[91]

A very different model has recently emerged in cases when a company's product cannot succeed without a "halo" of independent products for which it is the platform. The poster-child for this model is Apple's iPhone, whose success depends on thousands of independent developers of "apps." Once companies have created a market beachhead with a product, the creation of a partnership ecosystem can give their platform a longer life and make it more indispensable to the customer. Companies are thus spending more and more to attract and maintain these strong partnerships, which are typically not exclusive but rely on competition in the market-place. The importance of these partnerships is manifested by the lavish annual conferences or user group meetings that many companies now hold to promote their partnership ecosystem.

As discussed earlier, the era of corporate laboratories dedicated to basic research is over. However, some company laboratories, previously captive to the owning corporation's business, have evolved into resources available to industry at large. Xerox PARC, for example, has become the open-research model PARC, still a Xerox subsidiary but funded jointly by multiple industry partners (see Box 3-1). Some universities have taken on a similar role, partnering with consortia of funding companies that get a first look at the research breakthroughs or other special access, such as a non-exclusive license allowing them to then develop and build other proprietary products.

Many companies have created venture arms that invest in companies alongside pure venture investors or in venture funds as small limited partners. For example, Amgen has reduced its research spending but has invested in 26 companies through its own venture fund, beginning with at outlay of $100 million in 2004.[92] Many companies have created outreach groups that work with venture firms to find synergies between their products and the products of small venture-backed companies; these efforts may lead to product partnerships, corporate funding, or acquisition. A recent example is IBM's partnering with SignalDemand, with the IBM Venture Capital Group as the convener, to provide predictive analytics for ConAgra Mills, the third largest miller in North America and a grain industry leader.[93]

Partnerships between Industry and National Laboratories

U.S. industry enjoys significant support and encouragement to take advantage of collaborations with Federal and National laboratories. A legacy of Federal legislation has provided for access and opportunity to participate in the technology transfer program. This includes the Bayh-Dole Act, the Stevenson-Wyler Act, and the National Competitiveness Technology Transfer Act, which established technology as a mission of Federal R&D agencies. In the case of one of the key contributing elements, the DOE laboratories, the Energy Policy Act of 2005 gave specific impetus to technology transfer to support R&D in energy areas.

The principal coordinating entity for technology transfer is the Federal Laboratory Consortium for Technology Transfer (FLC). The FLC was organized in 1974 and consists of approximately 300 Federal laboratories and centers. Its objective is to "promote and facilitate rapid movement of Federal laboratory research results and technologies into the mainstream of the U.S. econo-my."[94] It allows prospective partners to identify technologies and areas of research where technology transfer agreements can be pursued.

As a leading example of the partnerships for technology transfer, the DOE has supported the engagement of its 17 National Laboratories and other technical centers with industry for the last two decades. There are many mechanisms for interaction. Cooperative Research and Development Agreements (CRADAs) can be executed between partners. User facilities are available for industry investigators in collaboration with laboratory scientists. Examples include the Combustion Research Facility of Sandia National Laboratories in Livermore, CA; the Advanced Photon Source at the Argonne

National Laboratory in Chicago, IL; and the Center for Nanophase Materials at the Oak Ridge National Laboratory in Oak Ridge, TN.

In addition to CRADAs and user facilities, Federal laboratories can participate in personnel exchanges, license intellectual property to industry, and fund agreements to support collaborative R&D with industry on a reimbursable basis. In 2008 the DOE laboratories executed 12,204 technology-transfer-related transactions, including 711 new CRADAs, 2530 WFO agreements involving non-Federal entities, 6146 licensing agreements, and 2817 user-facility agreements.[95] DOE laboratories reported $229.5 million in funding from non-Federal entities, $73.9 million from CRADA partners, and $49.3 in licensing income.

Emphasis on technology transfer came recently from a Presidential memorandum that called for acceleration of Federal technology transfer and commercialization, with major goals of adapting Federal R&D for use in the marketplace and supporting entrepreneurship based on Federal R&D.[96]

Among the many notable examples of successful research collaboration and technology transfer are a CRADA between the microelectronic industry and DOE laboratories to develop advanced lithography techniques, a longstanding partnership between the Goodyear company and Sandia National Laboratories for tire development, and a research alliance between Chevron and the Los Alamos National Laboratory (LANL) for advanced energy solutions. Partnerships may succeed in unlikely areas. For example, Proctor & Gamble (P&G), consummately a consumer product company, partnered with Los Alamos on the statistical modeling of manufacturing lines. P&G reports that it has realized more than $1 billion in production efficiency improvements.[97]

Looking forward, it is apparent that the Federal and National Laboratories represent a significant opportunity for U.S. industries. Cooperative research has overwhelmingly been shown to be effective in advancing the U.S. economy. The full potential of these collaborations and the utilization of unique facilities for cooperative research will not be realized, however, unless the process for establishing agreements is streamlined and made more effective in rapidly initiating research and achieving results.

Public-Private Partnerships between Industry and Government

Public-private partnerships are a means for meeting important national research needs in a way that includes private enterprise from the outset. The goal is to make the later transition from government to private funding not just easier, but self-propelled by the marketplace. We give just two examples here, while Chapter 4 goes into greater depth.

The first example is the Advanced Research Projects Agency–Energy (ARPA-E), established within DOE by the America COMPETES Act (2007) and intended to spur breakthrough energy-related research and technology transfer. ARPA-E has enabled both large and small companies to participate in innovation-centered government programs. The most recent round of awards, totaling $156 million of FY 2011 funds, included projects from 25 states; 50 percent were led by universities, 23 percent by small businesses, 12 percent by large businesses, 13 percent by National Laboratories, and 2 percent by nonprofits.[98]

The second example is the Biomarker Consortium, a pre-competitive collaboration in which companies and agencies jointly invest in early-stage research that benefits all. Members include the FDA, the NIH, Merck, Eli Lilly, GlaxoSmithKline, Roche, and others.[99] The objectives are to identify and validate new disease biomarkers (e.g., viral load in infectious disease, level of cholesterol in cardiac disease, molecular response in certain types of leukemia) for cases where the lack of such markers leads to prohibitively long treatment-development times and high costs.

These and other examples illustrate keys to success for public-private partnerships: focused research objectives, multi-sector partnerships, and pre-competitive collaborations that overcome market failures.

3.5. Summary: Where Are the Needs and Opportunities

In this chapter, we have described the profound effects that increased competition in the private sector and globalization are having on the U.S. research enterprise. In the next three chapters, we suggest some important paths forward. We will make the case that neither the Federal Government nor the universities themselves have fully recognized and responded to the changing role of universities, nor has industry been included in the discussion to the necessary extent, but that constructive opportunities abound. How can the partnership between the Federal funding agencies and the research universities be refounded to accommodate the new role of universities in the innovation ecosystem, while preserving their essential role in basic research? How can industry become more engaged in this process?

The next three chapters are built on three summary observations:

- First, universities are taking on a greater proportion of the early applied research formerly done in industrial laboratories, in addition to their traditional emphasis on fundamental research.
- Second, university graduates in science and engineering are entering a technology marketplace that is much more dynamic and more global than the one that existed 50 or even 20 years ago.
- Third, as subsequent chapters will explain, regulatory and reporting requirements on Federally-funded research have grown ever more burdensome, and reforms need to be enacted.

In our judgment, five key areas of opportunity follow from these observations, each implying multiple sets of useful actions that we will detail. The next three chapters are organized around these key opportunities and are stated as follows:

- Key Opportunity #1. The Nation has the opportunity to maintain its world-leading position in R&D investment, structured as a mutually supporting partnership among industry, the Federal Government, universities, and other governmental and private entities.
- Key Opportunity #2. The Federal Government has the opportunity to enhance its role as the enduring foundational investor in basic and early applied research in the United States. It can adopt policies that are most consistent with that role. Federal policy can seek to foster a sustainable R&D enterprise in which, when research is deemed worth supporting, it is supported for success.
- Key Opportunity #3. Federal agencies have the opportunity to grow portfolios that more strategically support a mix of evolutionary vs. revolutionary research; disciplinary vs. interdisciplinary work; and project-based vs. people-based awards.
- Key Opportunity #4. There is the opportunity for government to create additional policy encouragements and incentives for industry to invest in research, both on its own and in new partnerships with universities and National Laboratories.
- Key Opportunity #5. Research universities have the opportunity to strengthen and enhance their additional role as hubs of the innovation ecosystem. While maintaining the intellectual depth of their foundations in basic research, they can change their educational programs to better prepare their graduates to work in today's world.

They can become more proactive in transferring research results into the private sector.

IV. Maintaining Leadership and Reshaping Federal Roles

Key Opportunity #1. The Nation has the opportunity to maintain its world-leading position in R&D investment, structured as a mutually supporting partnership among industry, the Federal Government, universities, and other governmental and private entities.

In the previous chapter, we described the profound effects that increased private-sector competition and globalization are having on the U.S. research enterprise. In this chapter and the two following, we suggest some important paths forward. Neither the Federal Government nor the universities themselves have yet fully recognized and responded to the changing role of universities, nor has industry been included in the discussion to the necessary extent. How can the partnership between the Federal funding agencies and the research universities be re-shaped to take maximal advantage of the new role of universities in the innovation ecosystem, while preserving their essential role in basic research?

4.1. Magnitude and Stability of Investment in R&D

Action #1.1. PCAST recommends reaffirming the President's goal that total R&D expenditures should achieve and sustain a level of 3 percent of GDP. Congressional authorization committees should take ownership of pieces of that goal, with the Executive Branch and Congress establishing policies to enhance private industry's major share.

In Chapter 3, especially Figure 3-1, we saw that U.S. investments in R&D increasingly lag those of other countries as a percentage of their respective GDPs. The R&D investments of (as a percentage of GDP) Japan, South Korea, and Taiwan match or exceed those of the United States, with the last two continuing to increase. China's investment as a percentage of its GDP shows continuing, deliberate growth that, if it continues, should surpass the roughly flat United States investment within a decade, by which time China may also be the world's largest economy in terms of purchasing-power parity.[100] We see it as dangerous for the United States to be without a clearly articulated target for the overall magnitude of its R&D investment. The President's goal of 3 percent (including both Government and private investment) is not excessive. It is less than South Korea's and Japan's current value. We urge that this goal be forcefully reaffirmed.

Congressional authorization committees could also have important roles. They could identify as their individual responsibilities specific fractions of the 3 percent that fall within their jurisdiction, either as direct Federal investment (for those committees with jurisdiction over funding agencies), or else as sectors of private-sector investment that can be influenced by appropriate Federal policies (this for committees with jurisdiction over issues such as taxation, workforce, commerce, and immigration policy). Year-to-year tracking of changes in R&D investment at this level of granularity by the responsible authorization committees and with their continuing narrative, would provide valuable benchmarks. The White House Office of Science and Technology Policy, as the Federal S&T coordinating entity, also has an important, parallel role to play in monitoring the total R&D percentage investment and its allocation.

For 2009 (the latest available year for these statistics), U.S. R&D investment was 2.87% of GDP, having increased from a recent low of 2.55% in 2004. Unfortunately, this trend is in part misleading, since between 2008 and 2009 R&D investment actually *decreased*: the increase in percentage is an artifact of the decrease in U.S. GDP during the recession.[101] The President's goal of 3 percent especially needs to be achieved and sustained during the recovery, when the economic leverage of R&D investment may be largest.

Action #1.2. Recognizing its political difficulty, PCAST nevertheless urges Congress and the Executive Branch to find one or more mechanisms for increasing the stability and predictability of Federal research funding, including funding for research infrastructure and facilities. Possibilities include a cross-agency multiyear program and financial plan akin to DoD's Future Years Defense Program (FYDP) or multiyear appropriations for R&D.

From a historical perspective, the U.S. Government's commitment to the funding of science has been remarkably strong, and it has brought impressive results, in terms of continued U.S. leadership in publications, citations, Nobel Prizes, and significant discoveries, even in the face of rising competition. Yet the political process has inevitably led to an erratic, stop-and-go pattern of science funding. The NIH budget doubled from 1998 to 2003 and then declined 11.6 percent in real (inflation-adjusted) dollars over the next 5 years. In 2009-2010, the NIH budget temporarily increased again through the addition of the American Recovery and Reinvestment Act funds, but then continued to decline. The NSF budget was almost exactly flat in real terms between 2003 and 2008. President Obama, following on President Bush's pledge, stated his resolve to double it (in nominal terms) by 2016, but the U.S. financial and debt crises have rendered this goal difficult, if not impossible, to achieve on that time scale.[102] Defense and energy funding have been slightly less volatile, but still far from steady.

Such erratic patterns of funding, while superior to no growth at all, cause significant disruption in what is fundamentally a long-term activity. In periods of rapid expansion, offices and laboratories get overbuilt and Ph.D. production soars, leading to difficulties in fallow years. The 2009 American Recovery and Reinvestment Act (ARRA) delivered the largest increase in basic research funding in American history, more than $20 billion. But graduate students and postdoctoral fellows supported by these funds now face the question of how the next stages in their careers can be funded.

Yearly budget uncertainties cause significant and costly difficulties for construction and operation of large-scale science facilities such as accelerators, telescopes, and computing installations. These billion-dollar facilities are an essential component of the infrastructure needed for the physical, chemical, and biological disciplines. For example, accelerators are used to investigate the chemical and physical structure of nanomaterials, proteins, and medicines. By design, well-planned project schedules offer the lowest cost and shortest time to project completion. Unfortunately, yearly budget uncertainties often lead to nearly extemporaneous schedule modifications that delay and extend construction at considerable cost due to modified contracts and to the "standing-army" costs of maintaining continuity in personnel. In addition, constant replanning leads to significant management cost. Ensuring smooth and anticipated budgets will reduce the cost of the Nation's scientific facilities.

The Executive Branch (especially the Office of Management and Budget), along with Congress, needs to find mechanisms for ensuring a steadier, less volatile growth path for the long-term funding of science. Many of the decisions made by universities (to build labs, grant tenure, embark on a long-term research strategy as a department or research center) have lasting consequences. As one example, academic departments trying to determine the appropriate size of incoming classes of graduate students need to be able to project extramural research funding 5 years into the future, because that is how long it will take students, who are traditionally funded primarily on individual principal investigator grants, to get their degrees.

Federal research funding needs a mechanism akin to the DOD's Future Years Defense Program (FYDP), a program and financial plan that is approved annually by the Secretary of Defense. The FYDP arrays cost data, manpower, and force structure over a 6-year period for DOD internal review and then for program and budget review submission to OMB and the President.[103] It is also provided to Congress in conjunction with the President's budget. While its more distant out-years may represent only a notional commitment, the FYDP process generally succeeds in avoiding unrealistic wish lists for near-term years in favor of a plausible, executable plan. An initial, positive step would be for major R&D funding agencies like NIH and NSF to develop and submit to OMB and OSTP detailed, realistic multiyear planning budgets and for OMB and OSTP, after vetting these planning budgets for feasibility, to make them available to Congressional committees.

An even simpler measure would be to create multiyear appropriations for R&D, connected to the multiyear authorizations Congress has successfully implemented over the past few decades for nearly all R&D agencies. Indeed, the European Union's entire E.U.-wide research budget is appropriated 7 years at a time, which provides a desirable degree of predictability for European researchers. This idea is not new—over 30 years ago the General Accounting Office and Comptroller General (themselves arms of Congress, not the Executive Branch) noted the advantages of multiyear authorizations: "If R&D budgeting as a whole is to be improved, then a multiyear R&D appropriations process would also eventually need to be implemented."[104]

The specific nature of any new mechanism is less important than its predictability. We urge the Administration, especially OMB, and also the Congress to study these and other possible mechanisms for increasing the predictability of research funding.

4.2. Upgrade the Research and Experimentation Tax Credit

Action #1.3. The Research and Experimentation Tax Credit (usually called the R&D tax credit) needs to be made permanent. An increase in the rate of the alternative simplified credit from 14 percent to 20 percent would not be excessive. The credit also needs to be made more useful to small and medium enterprises that are R&D intensive by instituting any

or all of (1) refundable tax credits, (2) transferable tax credits, or (3) modifications in the definition of net operating loss to give advantage to R&D expenditures.

The Federal Research and Experimentation Tax Credit (often referred to as the R&D tax credit) was designed to encourage companies to develop new technologies by offsetting some of the financial risks inherent in R&D activities. Although the credit has served this purpose well in the 30 years since it was first enacted, it would be much more effective if it were made permanent, globally competitive, and reimbursable or transferable.

The current tax credit is a temporary measure that has been renewed 14 times since it was first enacted in 1981. It is widely viewed as having achieved its purpose of encouraging innovation at profitable, "advanced-stage" companies. These companies, with $250 million or more in gross receipts, claim about 80 percent of the total dollar value of R&D credit. Many companies use the Alternative Simplified Credit (ASC), which provides a credit equal to 14 percent of the current year's qualified research expenses that exceed 50 percent of the average qualified research expenses for the 3 preceding taxable years. In 2007 and 2008, tax credit claims were about $8.3 billion, with five industries accounting for about 75 percent: computer and electronic products; chemicals, including pharmaceuticals and medicines; transportation equipment, including motor vehicles and aerospace; information, including software; and professional, scientific, and technical services, including computer and R&D services.[105]

In 1981, when the United States began the Research and Experimentation Tax Credit program, it provided the greatest such incentive of any developed country. By 2008, however, the U.S. R&D credit ranked near the bottom of the 21 OECD countries offering such an incentive, and also lagged the incentives offered by China, India, Brazil, and Singapore.[106] One 2012 report ranks the United States 27th out of 42 countries studied in terms of R&D tax incentive generosity, down from 23rd just 5 years ago.[107]

Many countries are now providing refundable tax credits (i.e., the government directly pays companies the amount by which their credit exceeds their tax liability) as a way of providing incentives for innovation. The rationale for this is that many of the most disruptive and fundamental innovations come from small and medium enterprises (SMEs) that will have many years of losses and no taxable income and therefore derive no benefit from a nonrefundable tax credit. In industries that require a decade or longer before commercialization, such as in the health-care and alternative-energy sectors, this problem is particularly acute.

We reiterate the recommendation made by PCAST in its June 2011 report on Advanced Manufacturing, namely that the Federal Government should make permanent the Research and Experimentation Tax Credit.[108] Regarding the size of the credit, the economics literature does not suggest any sharp optimum. As discussed in Chapter 2, the support for innovation is both an economic decision and one of national character, priorities, and international competition. Thus viewed, an increase in the rate of the alternative simplified credit from 14 percent to 20 percent would not be excessive. According to one study, increasing the rate of the Alternative Simplified Credit (ASC) from 14 to 20 percent would increase annual GDP growth by $66 billion and create 162,000 jobs.[109] The Obama Administration's FY 2013 budget request for an increase to 17 percent is a good first step.[110] The certainty and support created by these changes would make companies more likely to include long-term R&D investments in their strategic plans.

We also recommend a thorough review of the Research and Experimentation Tax Credit to seek changes that would to make it more useful to SMEs that are R&D intensive—something akin to a "start-up innovation credit."[111] There are three principal means to achieve these goals: refundable tax credits, transferable tax credits, and revisions to modify definitions of net operating loss.

In general, transferability may be more possible to enact, because it is not directly accounted as a revenue loss. However, refunds are simpler and more direct, and because they involve fewer intermediaries would have a larger positive effect on the SMEs. While both refundable and transferable credits raise compliance issues, these are not qualitatively different from those of the existing system.

The existing Research and Experimentation Tax Credit can be carried forward for up to 20 years. Some have argued that because of this, as long as a start-up expects to be profitable within 20 years, the existing credit will create the desired incentive to undertake additional research now. The flaw with this argument is that most start-ups either fail or come close to failure. The line between success and failure is narrow and can be strongly influenced by the immediate affordability of research.

New capital is attracted to a start-up by the potential of its product, not by the discounted present value of its tax-credit carryover.

4.3. Adopt Policies That Allow Researchers to be Productive

Action #1.4. The Federal Government should adopt policies that increase the productivity of researchers, including more people-based awards, larger and longer awards for some merit-selected investigators, and administratively efficient grant mechanisms.

In the next section, Section 4.4, we will suggest ways to reduce unproductive cost burdens on universities as institutions. However, it is even more important to reduce the burdens on individual faculty principal investigators and others who actually conduct Federally sponsored research. These costs are hidden and therefore easy to overlook. They come out of the time of the researchers. They make research less productive. Researchers accomplish less research per Federal dollar than they otherwise might.

One recent study found that of the time that faculty devote to Federally sponsored research, 42 percent is spent on administrative tasks, and therefore not on conducting actual research.[112] Of this 42 percent, about half is spent on pre-award activities such as writing and submitting proposals and budgets, applying for approvals, and developing protocols, safety and security plans; and about half is spent on post-award activities, including grant progress report submissions, project revenue management, and institutional review board (IRB) compliance.

All these activities are a necessary part of research. The problem is not that that the Nation's research scientists are doing these activities. Rather, it is that they are doing them duplicatively, too often, and via too many different mechanisms across Federal agencies.

In the United States, all scientists, regardless of their position or institution, may apply for support of an innovative idea. This system embodies the ideal of a meritocracy, encouraging innovation to flower everywhere. When the number of applications for Federal research support in a particular field grows faster than available funding, success rates for proposals will drop. Indeed, this is what has occurred over the past three decades at NSF and NIH. From 2001 to 2011, for example, the overall research grant proposal success rate at NIH dropped from 32.1 percent to 17.7 percent.[113] Success rates within NSF Directorates or NIH Divisions likewise have a strong inverse correlation with the numbers of proposals submitted, which have risen sharply.

A result is a downward spiral of increasing numbers of proposal applications (imposing a growing burden on agencies' merit-review processes), decreasing success rates, and increasing non-productive pre-and post-award administrative burdens on the most creative and productive researchers at all career stages (but especially early career).

Action by government agencies is needed to break out of the spiral. If the Federal Government is to be the foundational investor in research, as we suggest in Key Opportunity #2, then it is not in the Government's interest to unproductively burden the very people in whom it is investing. In the next section, we put forth the principle that when research is deemed worthy of supporting, it should be supported to maximize success. This same principle holds for both institutions and people. Some agencies have tried some of the following actions to reduce pre-and post-award burdens on researchers to a limited extent, but much more aggressive efforts are needed to achieve future successes:

- More people-based, as distinct from project-based, awards, especially for basic research. For early career investigators, more awards like those in the NSF CAREER program, based on the promise of the investigator. For investigators at other career stages, more programs with awards based on the demonstrated productivity of the investigator, or of the laboratory or group that they supervise.
- Larger award sizes, and longer duration grants, for some merit-selected individual investigator grants, even if this means a decrease in overall proposal success rates.
- More award mechanisms that enable researchers to form administratively efficient groups of collaborating principal investigators more rapidly. In the size range that is smaller than a full-scale "center" but larger than a single investigator, there are opportunities for reducing the administrative burden on self-organizing groups of participants. NIH's encouragement of team science in this regard is exemplary.[114]

These recommendations are not contingent on overall growth of Federal support, but rather are directed toward increasing the efficiency of Federally supported research at any available level of support.

4.4. Foster a Sustainable Research Enterprise

Key Opportunity #2. The Federal Government has the opportunity to enhance its role as the enduring foundational investor in basic and early

applied research in the United States. It should adopt policies that are most consistent with that role. Federal policy can seek to foster a sustainable R&D enterprise in which, when research is deemed worth supporting, it is supported for success.

The Government-university partnership forged after World War II has been a critical element in U.S. leadership in science and technology over the last 60 years. Some aspects of that partnership have become discordant, however, while others have become rigid and averse to change. The deep bond between Government and the universities is still sound and should not be discarded. It is time to renew this government-university partnership for the next 50 years, and consequentially, changes in the global environment for research mean that the nature of the partnership must adapt.

The necessary and appropriate role of the Federal Government is easy to state: *It should be the enduring foundational investor in basic and early applied research in the United States.* We use the term "investor" advisedly. Investors provide resources, but only selectively and after careful review of a range of investment opportunities. Investors demand accountability from the management of enterprises in which they invest, but they are not themselves the managers of those enterprises. Looking at the Government-university partnership through this lens, we can identify several areas in need of improvement.

Action #2.1. The Federal Government should identify and achieve regulatory policy reforms, particularly relating to the regulatory burdens on research universities.

Research is done at the frontiers of human knowledge, often using specialized and novel methods, processes, and technologies that are not common in daily life or even in daily industrial life. Research must therefore conform to the highest standards of ethics, safety, and accountability. Research universities confront, and must live up to, these standards in a long list of areas that come under explicit Federal regulation and policies: human subjects, animal research, hazardous materials, select toxins and agents, conflict of interest and research integrity, financial reporting, export controls, and more.[115]

It is proper that universities should be accountable in all these areas. At the same time, it is important for the Federal Government to promote efficiency as universities strive to meet these responsibilities. Government's role is to maintain a regulatory and policy environment for research that properly balances the costs and benefits of regulations. It is PCAST's view that the United States is not doing a good job in that respect. Over the last two decades, the Government has added a steady stream of new compliance and reporting requirements, many of which vastly increase the flow of paper without causing any improvements in actual performance. Sometimes these requirements stand in the way of performance improvements.

While Executive Order 13563, "Improving Regulation and Regulatory Review," issued by President Obama on January 18, 2011, seeks to lower regulatory burdens broadly across the entire economy, research universities are unique in operating at the nexus of many different regulatory and policy regimes (some applying to them only) and more than 25 separate funding agencies.[116] As this report emphasizes, they also stand at the central locus of the new innovation ecosystem. For these reasons, they require special attention in the area of regulatory and policy reform.

Universities' responsibility to abide by prudent, safe, ethical, and lawful standards of behavior could be met at lower cost and with much less unproductive effort, while still reducing the actual risks associated with research to a minimum. A number of organizations, including the Association of American Universities, Association of Public and Land-grant Universities, the Council on Governmental Relations, and the National Research Council, have made detailed and actionable recommendations for how this goal could be achieved.[117] There is a broad consensus on actions that should be taken, which include the following:

- Elimination of regulations that do not add value or enhance accountability. The most glaring examples are effort-reporting and cost-accounting standards.[118]
- Ensuring that policies and regulations are meeting their goals in terms of performance, rather than simply in terms of process. Policies should reward best practices rather than punish technical or inconsequential anomalies. We note that successful quality-management systems in industry are virtually never "compliance regimes," but rather are systems that encourage self-assessment and documented, best-practice processes.[119]
- Harmonizing policies among agencies and statutes and eliminating unnecessary duplication.

- Simplifying sub-recipient monitoring requirements, especially when those sub-recipients are themselves universities already subject to Federal monitoring.
- Within the constraints of the Inspector General Act, reinforcing the original intent of the Single Audit Act by prohibiting audits and reviews that substantially duplicate the annual A-133 audit that each university undergoes. An official within OMB should be designated with authority to decide whether a proposed agency activity is duplicative.
- Amending the Regulatory Flexibility Act (RFA), which requires certain protections of small entities, to include not-for-profit organizations engaged in Federally sponsored research. The RFA encourages "tiering" of government regulations (by which different levels of regulation apply to different kinds of entities) or the identification of "significant alternatives" designed to make proposed rules less burdensome.
- Extending coverage under the Unfunded Mandates Reform Act (UMRA) to research universities, and allowing institutions to better account for new regulatory and grant management and reporting policy costs and to charge these costs to Federal awards.

By eliminating unproductive oversight, these changes can reduce costs to the Government on both the university side and on the Government side.

Action #2.2. The Federal agencies should appropriately circumscribe the use of cost sharing.

Almost by definition, universities share the cost of accomplishing Federally sponsored research. They hire faculty, recruit students, solicit gifts from alumni, and are generally responsible for creating the platform that makes sponsored research possible. In most cases, the full academic year salary of faculty is paid by the university even though the faculty member is expected to spend considerable time performing and supervising research. As used in this section, however, the term "cost sharing" refers to a particular set of practices by which a Federal agency sponsors a specific project or program but does not bear its full cost. The shortfall is made up, one way or another, by the institution receiving the Federal award.

Cost sharing was little used for most of the post-World War II period, but became more common in the 1980s and was codified in OMB Circular A-110 in 1993.[120] Cost sharing may be mandatory (required by the sponsor as a condition of obtaining an award), or it may be "voluntary committed," that is, included in a proposal budget as a binding commitment on the university's part and taken into consideration in the proposal's merit review. Different Federal agencies, and different programs within a single agency, may utilize either or both types of cost sharing and in variable amounts.

Cost sharing is often seen as offering two advantages. First, as a prudent investor, the Federal Government wants to ensure that a university partner has a level of commitment that will improve the prospects of success and perhaps compel university management attention better than (inappropriate) micromanagement from the Federal side. Second, Federal research agencies typically have ambitions that exceed their budgets; here, cost sharing can be seen as allowing program managers to approve more research projects than their agency can fully fund.

Our view is that both of these advantages are questionable and that cost sharing, used as a blunt instrument in service of two different goals, has unintended negative effects that usually exceed its value. Although statistical analysis of the first point would be hard (because few projects admit to bad management or failure), we are doubtful that cost sharing increases a project's probability of success. Once a university commits funds to cost sharing on a specific project, whether mandatory or "voluntary committed," the required expenditure is a sunk cost. As a general rule, the university does not improve its financial bottom line by better managing its committed cost share. While risk sharing may sometimes be a useful management tool, cost sharing, in practice, does not have this desired effect.

On the second point, the cost-sharing capacity of public universities that depend significantly on state support has dropped sharply in recent years. State appropriations to major public research universities per enrolled student dropped by 15 percent in just 2 years, from 2008 to 2010.[121] This sharp decline is part of a downward trend throughout the last decade. For example, the state general funds appropriated to the University of California per student has dropped from $15,020 in 2000–2001 to $6,770 in 2011–2012, in constant dollars.[122] A recent report of the National Science Board[123] calls attention to this trend more generally.

While it is rare (and politically unacceptable) for tuition revenues to be directly allocated to Federal cost sharing, just such a transfer is often the net effect of complicated puts and takes in budgets with a fixed or diminishing bottom line. Higher education funding cuts in Minnesota, for example, have caused approximately 9,400 students to lose their state financial aid grants entirely, while the remaining state financial aid recipients will see their grants cut by 19 percent.[124] Yet Minnesota must compete for Federal research dollars, including cost sharing, on the same terms as universities such as Stanford or MIT, which have little dependence on state support.

Collectively, universities are supporting research today to the tune of $11 billion nationwide.[125] Universities need to allocate their resources to fulfill their combined missions of education, research, and public service. They should not be taxing other critical parts of the university mission to support Federally funded research. The amounts in question are not small—research cost sharing by universities is equivalent to about one-third of their tuition revenues.[126]

Recognizing these and other problems, the National Science Board (NSB) in 2009 recommended narrowly circumscribing the application of mandatory cost-sharing requirements to NSF programs where cost sharing was foundational to achieving programmatic goals, and prohibiting mandatory and voluntary committed cost sharing in all other cases.[127] The NSB expressed the strong belief that its recommendations, which have been implemented by NSF,

> will not reduce institutional commitment and financial contributions to NSF-sponsored projects or negatively impact institutional stewardship of Federal resources. Instead, it likely will enhance the ability of institutions to strategically and flexibly plan, invest in, and conduct research projects and programs, and will promote equity among grantee institutions in NSF funding competitions.[128]

PCAST endorses the NSB recommendations and their implementation by NSF. We recommend that other funding agencies that currently implement cost sharing adopt similar policy changes or that the change be made Government-wide by OMB. Except in very special circumstances (such as explicit public-private partnerships; see Chapter 3), the goal of the Federal Government, as the foundational investor, should be to create a sustainable enterprise in which when research is deemed worth supporting, it is fully supported for success. In the interest of their own success, universities will continue to focus their resources (e.g., facilities and hiring) in areas where they believe they can make a difference.

We also recommend that cost-sharing policies for Federal awards should clearly differentiate between universities and for-profit entities that have a commercial stake in technology development. As one example, the DOE generally requires that institutions provide 20 percent of the Federally funded amount for R&D projects funded by the DOE technology offices.[129] In many cases this requirement prevents university researchers from participating. The 2010 PCAST Energy Report[130] recommended that the Administration should work to eliminate matching requirements for nonprofit entities in applied-energy research programs. Also, small business start-ups should be given up to 6 months after an award to acquire matching funds of 10 percent. We endorse these recommendations and think that they should analogously apply to all relevant Federal agencies.

4.5. Adopt More Active Portfolio Management as to Kinds of Research

Key Opportunity #3. Federal agencies have the opportunity to grow portfolios that more strategically support a mix of evolutionary vs. revolutionary research; disciplinary vs. inter-disciplinary work; and project-based vs. people-based awards.

The U.S. research enterprise must serve a complex mix of goals. This report emphasizes the du-al mandates of long-range investment in the foundations of basic and early applied research and in reducing the barriers for that research to give rise to new products, industries, and jobs. Federal agencies that fund research have their own mix of objectives and emphases. NSF, NIH, and DOE have responsibility for the majority of basic research, but the last two agencies also have specific mandates in health and energy, respectively. The Defense Advanced Research Projects Agency (DARPA) has national security as its prime objective.

At the national level, the United States practices a kind of portfolio management, meaning that the Government seeks to optimize a combination of objectives through an appropriate mix of strategies to achieve the goals noted above. As has long been understood by economists and game theorists, an optimized mixture produces on average better results than any single strategy might do. Part of this portfolio management lies with Congress and is therefore mediated by a broad, if sometimes frustrating, political process. Another more formal part resides in the Executive Branch, specifically within OMB.

At the level of individual funding agencies, principles of portfolio management are practiced across the fields and subfields for which the agencies have responsibility. Inputs to this complex process include Congressional direction; national needs and Administration initiatives; studies by the National Research Council and other bodies; and the shared sense of the scientific community at large of what is new, exciting, important, or promising.

In part a consequence of the global changes that were described in Chapter 3, research is increasingly distinguished not just by its field, such as "immunology" or "chemical engineering," but also by its type or character, for example:

- *Evolutionary* (also called *incremental*) versus *revolutionary* (also called *transformative* or *high-risk, high-return*).[131]
- *Disciplinary*, meaning that it fits well into existing institutional structures such as academic departments or degree programs, versus *interdisciplinary*, meaning that it is not such a good fit, usually because skills from several different disciplines are utilized.
- *Project-based*, meaning that a particular scientific discovery, described in advance, is within reach, versus *people-based*, meaning that a person or team is deemed worthy of support on the basis of their documented promise and ability or recent previous record of success.

These are only three of several possible axes, but we think they are the most important three. Just these three give eight possible combinations of the axes, descriptors such as "evolutionary, interdisciplinary, and people-based." While each axis is defined as a dichotomy, in truth each is a continuous spectrum, so we speak of the eight combinations as rough descriptions, not as a strict classification.

All eight combinations describe valid and important kinds of scientific research. Indeed, science would be hobbled if research were restricted to any one, or a small number, of the combinations. What is needed is strategic portfolio management across all eight.

Therein lies a serious present deficiency, recognized not only in this report, but in many previous studies and also internally by funding agencies directors and career staff.[132] That is, despite previous reforms, the research sponsored by most agencies can be characterized by one, or perhaps two, dominant combinations – though different from agency to agency. For example, it is widely recognized that the vast majority of NIH and NSF awards (see the following statistics for the exceptions) are *evolutionary, disciplinary, and project-based.* NIH and NSF also see themselves as having a special responsibility toward single-investigator-led science (R01 grants at NIH and single-PI grants at NSF).

The 2008 ARISE report describes a "troubling consensus" that Federal agencies, "systematically shy away from high-risk projects," and it recommends that agencies adopt funding mechanisms and policies that nurture transformative research in *all* award programs.[133] In a 2007 report, the National Science Board noted a similar problem: "it is unreasonable to expect that small adjustments to NSF's existing programs and processes will overcome the perception … that iconoclastic ideas are not welcome at NSF."[134] In response, NSF's latest strategic plan urges new emphasis on interdisciplinary, high-risk, and potentially transformative research and education.[135]

DARPA, as a notable exception, adopts a model that emphasizes intense short-term forays into uncharted territory beyond the recognized scientific frontier. DARPA's combinations are *revolutionary*, either *disciplinary* or *interdisciplinary*, and *project-based*. These projects often fail, but when they succeed, they can produce spectacular results. But in its different corner, DARPA appears equally wedded to a one-or two-combination model. In some cases, its mission might be better served by a broader, managed portfolio.

PCAST feels strongly that the needs of the U.S. S&T enterprise are not best served by a single dominant model of research within each agency.

Action #3.1. Each agency should have a strategic plan that explicitly addresses the different kinds of research activities that can contribute to its mission, specifically addressing the axes of evolutionary vs. revolutionary research; disciplinary vs. interdisciplinary work; and project-based vs. people-based awards.

There is no need for every agency to support every combination of research axes. Instead, the need is for a process within each agency that is transparent and strategic, based on its present and future mission rather than on traditional ways of doing business. For NIH and NSF, we would be surprised if such a process did not yield a significantly increased portfolio among the underrepresented combinations that are not *evolutionary* and *disciplinary projects*. We recommend that, with coordination from OSTP and OMB, each agency publish, in a common format, its strategic plan, including its rationale for resource allocations among the eight combinations, and the amounts so allocated.

What do such allocations look like now? NSF and NIH have recognized the need for each to fund more *revolutionary* research, and each has initiated specific programs with this goal.[136] Such programs at NIH include the NIH

Director's Pioneer Award (NDPA), the NIH Director's New Innovator Award (NIA), the NIH Director's Early Independence Award (EIA), and the NIH Director's Transformative R01 awards. These are all funded from the NIH Common Fund (crosscutting across the Institutes). In addition, the individual institutes award so-called Avant-Guard and EUREKA grants by the traditional (and dominant) R01 review mechanism. At NSF, the previous Small Grants for Exploratory Research (SGER) program was expanded and replaced by two mechanisms that only require internal review, the Grants for Rapid Response Research (RAPID) program and the Early-concept Grants for Exploratory Research (EAGER) program. In November 2011, NSF announced new Creative Research Awards for Transformative Interdisciplinary Ventures (CREATIV), budgeted for $24 million.

While this plethora of initiatives, each worthy in its own way, gives an illusion of significant progress, in truth the sum of all of these programs is tiny, almost invisible, in comparison to each agency's dominant model. For example, in 2004, the first year of the NDPA awards, just 9 of 1300 applications were funded. Three years later, the number funded had risen to 20.[137] However, in 2012, only 7 NDPA awards, 33 NIA awards, and 10 EIA awards are expected.[138] For comparison, NIH expects to make 35,944 total research grants in FY2012.[139] While these awards provide useful recognition to their recipients, they are but a drop in the bucket of total agency funding. Although NSF is congressionally authorized to fund up to 5 percent of its budget for high-risk, high-reward research, in FY2011 the relatively mature RAPID and EAGER programs comprised 2.8 percent of new NSF research grant funding. For FY2012, the CREATIV program, a pilot grant mechanisms under the Integrated NSF Support Promoting Interdisciplinary Research and Education (INSPIRE) initiative that is replacing RAPID AND EAGER, is funded at less than half a percent of the NSF total budget. At NIH, FY2012 total funding of the individual NDPA, NIA, EIA, Transformative R01, Avant-Guard, and EUREKA programs is less than 3 percent of new awards and less than 0.5 percent of all research project grants (including new awards).[140]

In addition to specific programs focused on supporting new and emerging areas of research, agencies have developed review criteria and other policies to target funding for ground-breaking, high-reward projects. In our estimation, however, none of these has been sufficient to the magnitude of the problem. We call for a substantially larger effort to support research proposals (1) with potential game-changing impact; (2) that fall outside traditional disciplines; and (3) that are people, rather than project, based.

Action #3.2. Each agency should diversify its mechanisms for merit review to be optimal for the portfolio in its strategic plan.

A key part of each strategic plan should be the agency's path toward adopting an appropriately diverse set of merit-review mechanisms, one optimized for its mix of research among multiple combinations, as previously defined.

Although there are good reasons for different agencies to tailor their merit-review processes to their particular goals and missions. However, there has historically been a centripetal convergence within agencies on a single dominant review model, optimized for the dominant kind of research. This impedes necessary progress toward diversity in more axes of research.

The form of merit review varies greatly across agencies and programs. Some agencies, such as NSF and NIH, rely heavily on panels of scientists from outside the agency to evaluate and rank the proposals, frequently with the help of advice from additional reviews of the proposals by individual scientists. In this model, government staff officers oversee the process by, for example, selecting reviewers and panel members. At both NSF and NIH, program directors have some albeit limited discretionary powers. NSF program directors, for example, may use their own professional judgment in cases where there is a sharp divergence of opinion by a review panel – potentially indicating a revolutionary, but risky, proposal.[141] Both NSF and NIH may also weigh factors such as capacity building and special program objectives into their decisions. By and large, however, when outside review panels are used, awards are made according to their ranking of proposals, a procedure that NIH refers to as a "payline."[142]

Other agencies and programs, such as DOE Basic Energy Sciences, use peer review to help program managers make decisions, but it is the program manager or office director who makes the funding decision. In more mission-driven and applied-research programs, such as DARPA or the Office of Naval Research (ONR), the merit-review process may be done internally, with nongovernment reviews solicited ad hoc only when they are perceived to be needed. In this case, the program manager plays a dominant role in making funding decisions. A model that works well for DARPA is to recruit into *non-renewable* term positions visionary program executives who are given predictable budgets and the authority to act, with minimal programmatic oversight, as decision-makers. NSF allows program officers to allocate up to 5% of their program budgets using internal review of proposals (subject to limits on the size of individual award budgets), provided that these are for exploratory, high-risk ideas or for research activities that requires a rapid response to a transient opportunity such as a natural event.

A 2010 review of different kinds of merit review commissioned by DOE's Office of Energy Efficiency and Renewable Energy (EERE) distinguished between agencies that focus on basic research, where exploration and fundamental knowledge are a critical goal, and agencies that conduct mission-driven or applied research, where specific deliverables, cost goals, and time scales are critical.[143] This distinction is important, but many programs and agencies support research that cuts across this divide. Indeed, many research efforts may have basic and applied goals that can be pursued simultaneously. Such classification is useful in determining what style of merit review is most appropriate for the program goals, however.

Each of the different models for merit review described in the EERE report has strengths and weaknesses. A common criticism of the study panel or review panel (at NIH or NSF), for example, is that these panels tend to give relatively conservative advice to their convening programs, recommending proposals that attract the most uniform praise and rejecting those that generate controversy. This may lead to supporting science that is more evolutionary in nature, although still of high quality, rather than riskier science that may sometimes have higher impact.

To some extent, the conservatism of review panels is compensated for by individual researchers. If researchers know that panels will make review recommendations in this manner, they tend not to submit proposals that describe risky research plans, instead proposing evolutionary research that has a high likelihood of success and then, to the extent allowed by agency regulations, using small portions of their grant to support new, riskier projects. Few would argue, however, that this should be the way that high-risk, high-impact research should be supported as a matter of national policy.

Models of merit review that depend much more on the decisions of individual program managers or directors are able to make less conservative decisions and can be more nimble in supporting new areas. But these models also face challenges. Some programs that operate in this manner have a reputation for insularity, in which longtime relationships between researchers and program managers are thought to be important in the funding decisions. Once a researcher has "broken in" to the particular program and has received support for his or her research, there is an expectation in some programs that this support will continue unless there is a substantial change in research direction or research quality. Any perception of unfairness can harm the effectiveness of the overall enterprise, discouraging new researchers from applying and decreasing the intensity of the competition.

On the other hand, for many mission-driven agencies or programs, these concerns are more than offset by the positive effect this system has in selecting the most exciting research projects that can lead to large impacts. In addition, there can sometimes be a good rationale for providing long-term, continuing support to a group of researchers with demonstrated records of high achievement.

In models where program manager judgment dominates, it is important to incorporate the periodic use of an external panel that retrospectively reviews a manager's decisions to ensure that access to the funding pool for new researchers was not restricted and that the best new ideas were supported, not just those from an established pool of investigators.

Action #3.3. Each agency should adopt policies that increase the agility of funding new fields, unexpected opportunities, and the creativity of new researchers.

A concern for all funding agencies, whatever the style of merit review they employ, is that scientific communities can be slow to embrace new approaches and paradigms. New ideas may fall outside the boundaries of established programs or panels and thus fall between the cracks. Even programs such as DARPA or ARPA-E that are designed to identify novel, risky but impactful ideas may fail to recognize the most exciting new research directions in their early stages.

It is important to ensure that structural barriers do not impede the emergence of new fields. This includes considering how study section boundaries and tenure criteria affect the review of proposals in new disciplinary areas. The present situation at NIH and NSF is far from ideal.

Similarly, while agencies already take measures to ensure that new and early career researchers are not disadvantaged in merit review, we think that much more needs to be done. Not only should early career researchers not be *disadvantaged*, but explicit recognition should also be given to the fact that new scientists, in particular graduate students and post-doctoral researchers, bring a unique kind of creativity to their fields. Wherever possible, that creativity needs to be unleashed. Instead of restricting graduate students to a particular project or laboratory by providing their funding through a larger research grant, increased graduate fellowships or training grants could give graduate students the freedom to choose their research focus. Such an emphasis on fellowships or training grants would utilize the enthusiasm of students to recognize exciting research in early stages.

Post-doctoral fellowship programs can also play an important role in a system designed to encourage innovation. Programs that provide support for early-career scientists with demonstrated potential, along with programs for mid-career and more senior scientists with demonstrated records of achievement, could also accelerate innovation by supporting individuals instead of projects.

Such efforts do not circumvent the merit-review process. By focusing on the individual, these efforts simply shift the question asked of merit review from "what is the best project?" to "who is most likely to develop new ideas?"

There is no single approach that is universally appropriate. Mission-driven agencies might fund training grants in particular areas, such as renewable energy or satellite design; basic research agencies such as NSF might emphasize fellowships awarded to individuals, such as their existing graduate fellowship program.

In both cases, moving some support for graduate students from research grants to training grants and fellowships is likely to accelerate the support for new ideas and new research directions by recognizing the general bias of the merit-review process for more evolutionary research.

There are existing programs at NIH and NSF that already seek to address the above concerns and opportunities. NIH programs include Career Transition Awards (K22), Mentored Research Scientist Development Awards (K01), Independent Scientist Awards (K02), and Pathway to Independence Awards K99/R00. In FY11, funding for all K awards (including some highly targeted programs not relevant to our concerns here) totaled 2.1 percent of NIH funding.

At NSF, the successful CAREER program, whose awardees are considered to be the elite of young American science in NSF-funded fields, commands just 2.8 percent of NSF's FY12 budget.[144]

In June 2007, NIH Director Zerhouni established a formal effort to improve peer review practices within NIH. With advice from external and internal advisory panels, this "Enhancing Peer Review Initiative" led in 2008 to several changes in NIH review procedures, including:[145]

- A mandate that reviewers provide an "overall impact" score for each proposal reviewed. (NOT-OD-09-025).
- A change in the scoring scale from the old system of 1 to 5 in increments of 0.1 to a new system of 1 to 9 in increments of 1, along

with the mandate that proposals be separately scored for "significance, investigator(s), innovation, approach, and environment" (NOT-OD-09-024).

- The provision of fillable templates, so that reviewers could provide their reviews more easily and uniformly.
- The formal identification of new and early career applicants (ESIs). "It is hoped that by providing an advantage for [that is, merely identifying] ESIs, the NIH will be able to directly encourage earlier application for NIH research grant support" (NOT-OD-08-121).

Resulting as they did from an extended public process with much outside visibility and participation, these arguably rather small and bureaucratic changes strengthened the views of some skeptics of internally driven change at NIH.[146]

Soon afterward, however, some teeth were put into the measures designed to encourage new and early career applications with the policy announcement, "NIH intends to support new investigators at success rates comparable to those for established investigators submitting new applications."[147] In other words, recognizing that early career investigators were, de facto, being disadvantaged by the existing peer-review process, their share of resources would be adjusted to success-rate parity with established investigators.

We find much to commend in this approach in the context of need for immediate progress on a vexing issue. Instead of mere encouragement, this approach, when followed, actually produces necessary change in the allocation of resources.

However, it is a blunt tool that corrects an inadequate peer-review mechanism at the output side, after it has acted. What is needed, as suggested by Action #3.2, is a portfolio of significantly different peer-review mechanisms, matched to an explicit strategic plan for supporting different kinds, or combinations, of research.

One or more of these different mechanisms should be designed from the ground up (differently from existing study section panels) to identify and fund the creativity of new and early-career researchers at significant levels.

The problem is not that the need for early-career support is unrecognized. It is that efforts to address the need have been, in our view, inadequate in magnitude.

V. PROVIDING A BETTER POLICY ENVIRONMENT FOR INDUSTRY

Key Opportunity #4. There is the opportunity for the Government to create additional policy encouragements and incentives for industry to invest in research, both on its own and in new partnerships with universities and National Laboratories.

Industry is uniquely able to adopt the inventions and discoveries of scientific research and from them generate high-quality jobs by investing its capital in the Nation's future. If innovative technology companies are to serve in this role, however, they need to operate in an environment that encourages and rewards technology entrepreneurship. An important element of this environment is a set of government policies that (1) encourages companies to develop competitive products based on new technologies and (2) helps to train and educate the skilled work-force such companies need to succeed in the competitive global markets of today and the future. This does not require Government to micromanage the relationships between universities and industries, which are already well developed and growing steadily stronger. Rather, it requires a framework of carefully considered policies in the following areas: science education, immigration of technology workers, intellectual-property rights, R&D tax credits, export controls, and in appropriate circumstances, seed funding for companies performing applied research.

In this chapter we discuss ways in which the government, with a few targeted policy changes, can improve the national research environment and speed the progress of industrial innovation. Some of these recommendations directly apply to increasing the ability of industry to support research and development, and others apply more broadly.

5.1. Provide a Larger and Better Technological Workforce

For U.S. technology companies to be the world's strongest, they need a continuing flow of world-leading scientists, engineers, and technology managers. For decades, the United States has filled this need in two ways: by educating and motivating top students in the United States and by attracting the best and brightest from around the world. Today, however, the rest of the developed (and developing) world is equally determined to create a skilled workforce and to equal or surpass the United States in recruitment strategies. If the United States is to sustain the leadership quality of its workforce, it needs to redouble its effort on three fronts: K-12 STEM education, university education, and recruitment of highly-skilled foreign workers and students. Research universities have key roles in all three strategies because of their ability to integrate research and education at both undergraduate and graduate levels.[148]

Action #4.1. Improve STEM education so as to produce more and better home-grown researchers and technology entrepreneurs.

PCAST's September 2010 report on kindergarten through grade 12 (K-12) STEM education articulates the importance of getting STEM education right: "STEM education will determine whether the United States will remain a leader among nations and whether we will be able to solve immense challenges in such areas as energy, health, environmental protection, and national security."[149] We strongly endorse the recommendations and conclusions of that report and reiterate that nothing is more important to the future health of the research enterprise of this country.

Universities are increasingly recognizing the need to assess the quality of their undergraduate STEM education and to encourage adoption of teaching methods that are the most effective. We encourage this trend. Acknowledging the proposals laid out in PCAST's February 2012 report on improving undergraduate STEM education in the first 2 years of college, the Association of American Universities (AAU) recently launched a 5-year initiative for improving undergraduate STEM education, including increasing retention of students in STEM degrees by improving introductory STEM teaching.[150] Currently, about 60 percent of students who plan to major in STEM fields switch to non-STEM fields before graduation.[151] The AAU emphasized that active-learning techniques have proved to be more engaging and inspiring and more effective at helping students learn and called for their implementation. One troubling trend among financially stressed public institutions is differential (higher) tuition charged to STEM majors, a practice that makes it even harder to attract talented students to STEM fields, especially those from economically disadvantaged backgrounds.[152] This is talent that we cannot afford to lose.

The U.S. science and technology enterprise has always benefited from what are widely regarded as the strongest science and engineering graduate programs in the world. To take full advantage of these programs, large technology companies are increasingly incorporating work-force development as a feature of their university partnerships. In addition to funding research, the companies now support more graduate fellowships.

Universities are also taking a more explicit role in training tech-savvy entrepreneurs to start and grow the companies capable of developing disruptive technologies. We also encourage this trend. Researchers who may become the founders of new companies need an understanding of business principles. It is important to engage them in the world of entrepreneurship early in their career. Some research universities, as described in Section 3.3, are developing new programs to meet this need, and more should be developed.

Action #4.2. Attract and retain, both for universities and industry, the world's best researchers and students from abroad.

Even positing improvements in attracting and retaining the best students in STEM disciplines domestically, technology-based firms will need to continue to attract a significant fraction of the most talented scientists and engineers from around the world. These people are needed not to replace but to complement the insufficient numbers of technically trained U.S. citizens. Highly skilled people from abroad bring not only their knowledge and talent to the U.S. research enterprise, they can also be the glue that binds the international collaborations that increasingly define the global R&D landscape.

Consider these statistics:

- Immigrants are nearly 30 percent more likely to start a business in the United States than non-immigrants, and they represent 17 percent of all new business owners in the United States.[153]
- Immigrants represent 24 percent of U.S. scientists and 47 percent of U.S. engineers with bachelor's or doctorate degrees.[154]
- Immigrants have started 25 percent of U.S. public companies that were venture-backed—including Google, eBay, Yahoo, Sun Microsystems, and Intel. Immigrant-founded, venture-backed public companies employ 220,000 people in the United States.[155]

A generation ago, many of the best science and engineering students from around the world eagerly came to this country if they had the opportunity. This is less often true today. NSF Director Subra Suresh relates that 80 percent of his 1977 graduating class at the Indian Institutes of Technology received offers for graduate study in the United States, and virtually all came here—and stayed. On a recent visit to his alma mater, he learned that 80 percent of IIT graduates still receive U.S. offers, but only 16 percent accept them.[156]

Under current rules, foreign students can stay in the United States for 12 months after graduation for Optional Practical Training (OPT), that is, work experience in their field of study. Students with certain STEM degrees qualify for an extra 17-month OPT extension, to a total of 29 months, for the purpose of contributing to the U.S. economy. This also allows time for them to in some cases obtain an H-1B or other longer-term visa. In May 2011 and in May 2012, DHS issued an expanded list of fields eligible for the extension, among them neuroscience, medical informatics, drug design, mathematics, computational science, and computer science.[157] PCAST commends this process and urges that additional fields with positive economic impact be added to the list.

As a longer term fix, we strongly endorse the strategy recommended by two PCAST reports, the 2010 report on nanotechnology[158] and the 2011 report on advanced manufacturing, to encourage foreign students to both come to and remain in the United States:

> Expand the number of high-skilled foreign workers that may be employed by U.S. companies. This can be done by such policies as allowing foreign students who receive a graduate degree in STEM from a U.S. university to receive a green card, allowing each employment-based visa to automatically cover a worker and his or her spouse and children, and increasing the number of H-1B visas.[159]

Increasingly, foreign students in the United States have attractive options for returning home to develop their careers. If we want to keep the very best here, we need to make the career option of remaining in the United States not only possible, but desirable.

5.2. Fix Problems with Export Control

The control of certain exports is necessary to protect the security interests of the United States. Both the Export Administration Regulations (EAR) and the International Traffic in Arms Regulations (ITAR) address this need, requiring U.S. citizens to receive a license from the Federal Government before shipping abroad any technology or technical data identified on U.S. export-control lists. In addition, both the EAR and ITAR deem the release of such regulated information to foreign nationals in the United States to be an export to that person's country of nationality (the "deemed export" rule) and therefore prohibited.

Fundamental research activities at universities are in general excluded from export-control restrictions. This exclusion is based on President Reagan's National Security Decision Directive (NSDD) 189, which is still in force. The exemption for fundamental research is codified at 15 C.F.R. § 734.8.[160] The importance of maintaining the fundamental research exclusion was re-emphasized in a position memo sent in February 2011 to the Departments of Commerce and State by four associations representing universities and other research institutions:[161] "As recognized in NSDD 189, the free exchange of ideas is vital to our scientific leadership and creativity, upon which much of our national and economic security depends." PCAST agrees.

Sponsored research offices at universities screen grants or contracts to ensure that they include no export-control restrictions. Given the large numbers of foreign students and postdocs involved in research on U.S. campuses, it would be virtually impossible to perform such restricted research without violating the "deemed export" rule of the EAR and ITAR. This restriction represents a serious impediment to university-industry partnerships, since a company performing R&D in a defense or aerospace project, for example, is likely to require a great deal of export-controlled work. A university can participate in such a research partnership only by setting up an expensive off-campus facility with restricted access.

While there is no disagreement on the necessity of proper export controls to safeguard U.S. security, technology-based firms need a level playing field to export successfully at today's level of competition. Wes Bush, CEO and President of Northrop Grumman, has argued persuasively that export restrictions make it impossible for domestic companies to compete in the growing global market for unmanned aircraft—without making the country safer.[162] Such restrictions, for example, prevent companies from selling remote-piloted aircraft even to allies for any of their many nondefense applications. Bush points out that a similar regulation prevented U.S. companies from exporting satellite communications to allies. In response, other countries developed their own communications industries and produced "ITAR free" products locally.

Action #4.3. Support the President's Export Control Reform initiative and further measures.

To provide an improved regulatory network, the subcommittee on Export Administration (PECSA) of the President's Export Control Council (PCA) is working to implement the President's Export Control Reform (ECR) initiative. Major elements in the initial stages of the ECR initiative include grouping of controlled items on a single list, identifying a single agency to control export licensing, establishing a single modern IT system for export controls, and making improvements in education and enforcement.

PCAST endorses the ECR initiative and further steps that can lead to a more thoughtful and effective approach to export control. The principle of the proposed reform is to build very secure walls around a few sensitive technologies, rather than too many walls that may block desirable activities and weaken the nation's competitiveness. If enacted, the recommendations of the ECR initiative will release American defense and aerospace industries to compete globally without harming the national defense. At the same time, they may invite closer industry-university partnerships in areas of great potential importance to the national economy.

5.3. Make Stronger Connections between Industry and National Laboratories

Action #4.4. Enable streamlined interactions between U.S. National Laboratories and industry.

As described in Section 3.1, U.S. industry enjoys the advantage of being able to draw on unparalleled science and technology capacity, including the world's leading universities and the world's leading National Laboratories. Over the past three decades, industries have also made substantial progress in bringing university-generated technologies to the marketplace and in developing long-term university-industry research partnerships. Such progress has come more slowly at the U.S. National Laboratories, although significant progress has been made.

The Stevenson-Wydler Technology Innovation Act of 1980 stipulated that the Federal Government should try to transfer technology to the private sector whenever appropriate and that each National Laboratory establish an Office of Research and Technology Applications (ORTA). The Federal Technology

Transfer Act of 1986 went further in mandating that scientists and engineers at National Laboratories should take responsibility for technology transfer to the extent consistent with the laboratories' primary missions. This act created the Cooperative Research and Development Agreement (CRADA) as a mechanism that Government Owned-Government Operated (GOGO) laboratories could use to establish research partnerships. The statute also chartered the Federal Laboratory Consortium for Technology Transfer and required that each agency devote some of its budget to it. The National Competitiveness Technology Transfer Act of 1989 extended the CRADA mechanism to Government Owned-Contractor Operated Laboratories (GOCOs). Today, the primary direct mechanisms for transferring technology from the National Laboratories to industries are collaborative research agreements such as CRADAs, and licensing agreements that transfer laboratory inventions to both established and start-up companies.

It is relatively easy to find successful examples of technology transfer from the National Laboratories. Argonne National Laboratory announced two licensing agreements in January 2011 for the patented composite cathode material technology used in advanced lithiumion batteries for electric vehicles, one with General Motors and one with the company that plans to manufacture battery cells for the Chevy Volt.[163] Battelle Memorial Institute established a venture capital fund in 2003 that works closely with the ORTAs at the seven GOCO laboratories that Battelle manages or co-manages.[164] And the NIH Office of Technology Transfer Activities tracks the many FDA-approved products that were developed with technologies from the Intramural Research Program at the National Institutes of Health.[165]

However, evidence suggests that much of the laboratories' potential for collaborating with industry remains untapped. The Department of Commerce has released a study by the Science and Technology Policy Institute based on an extensive review of the literature and interviews with staff from 26 laboratories and 13 agencies over 6 months.[166] The authors reported that while "technology transfer and commercialization activities at Federal laboratories have evolved and grown over the last 30 years," many barriers remain. The report found that industry was generally unfamiliar with the laboratories and their potential value, and government rules and procedures discouraged collaboration. The report pointed out that "Federal Government and industry time scales still often differ," and the length of time to complete negotiation of an agreement continued to be a source of frustration.

PCAST believes that the full potential of industry-laboratory collaborations will not be realized unless the process for establishing agreements is streamlined and made more effective. Best practices from university-industry partnerships should be brought over to the university-laboratory environment to the extent that current law allows. Both the laboratories themselves and the Federal agencies that sponsor them need to show greater diligence on this important issue.

VI. Reshaping Policies for the Research Universities and Their Partnerships

Key Opportunity #5. Research universities have the opportunity to strengthen and enhance their additional role as hubs of the innovation ecosystem. While maintaining the intellectual depth of their foundations in basic research, they can change their educational programs to better prepare their graduates to work in today's world. They can become more proactive in transferring research results into the private sector.

6.1. Keeping U.S. Research Universities the Best in the World

Action #5.1. Maintain strong commitment to the scope and intellectual depth of fundamental university research.

The university has become the center for basic and early applied research. Billions of dollars from the Federal Government, philanthropists, foundations, and industry partners support a broad research platform that sustains faculty and their graduate students and postdoctoral fellows. In 2009, the Federal Government invested more than $32.6 billion in university-based research and development activities.[167]

We emphasized in Chapter 2 that fundamental research, carried out as a matter of scientific inquiry, has been the essential seed for the largest and most economically valuable innovations. This has been proved repeatedly over the last century. It is a central tenet of this report that U.S. universities have, and must continue to have, a foundational commitment to basic and fundamental research. Indeed, that commitment must be a research university's preeminent responsibility: to maintain the intellectual depth of its disciplinary fields and to encourage interdisciplinary ventures that can give rise to new areas for intellectual exploration.

It is also clear that universities are taking on an additional role as hubs of the innovation eco-systems. Because policies affecting this role have, to date, been less completely examined and discussed, most of the recommendations of this report are focused in this area. This does not mean, however, that universities should skew their reward and promotion processes toward departments or faculty whose interests seem to align most closely with this additional role. Such a distortion of universities' fundamental mission would, in the long run, undermine exactly the position as hubs of innovation that they need to occupy. In the following sections we describe how universities may grow into their new role, but we take it as a given that their responsibility both for research at the frontier and for the teaching of the next generation will not diminish.

6.2. Improving Education at U.S. Universities

Action #5.2. Augment the educational mission for today's world.

Especially in times of rapid global change, the educational practices of universities, in terms of what they teach and how they teach it, need frequent reexamination. Here, we highlight some aspects of curriculum that we think should all universities should provide.

With the evolution of STEM careers, graduate education is not well aligned with the breadth of America's workforce needs. In particular, doctoral education is focused primarily on research in a discipline, often leaving graduates insufficiently trained in many of the vital workforce skills necessary for success in the STEM professional workforce and critical to U.S. competitiveness in the 21st century. Examples of important skills that Ph.D.-level employees typically need, whether they are employed in academia or elsewhere, but for which most new Ph.Ds are ill prepared, include project management, leadership, communication, the ability to work in teams, the expertise to address complex interdisciplinary problems, and the ability to teach. Also important to future members of the workforce is an understanding of the essential roles of innovation and entrepreneurship in the 21st century workforce. These elements, essential to the nonacademic science and technology sectors, typically receive little attention in graduate school although these sectors are where the majority of Ph.Ds. will be employed.[168]

Academic institutions should prepare graduate students for the 21st century by providing expanded and enhanced opportunities to learn the skills needed for success in the full range of professional STEM career paths. Such graduate education modernization must be done without compromising the research enterprise that depends heavily on graduate students to advance knowledge and innovation. Federal agencies should provide incentives for increased educational opportunities. In partnership with academic institutions and industry, Federal agencies should develop program, funding, and policy modifications to enhance graduate education. The agencies should also develop evaluation strategies for these modifications and other related interventions to assess their impacts on graduate education and on the research enterprise. When not specific to a particular discipline or enterprise, these Federal efforts should be harmonized and integrated across agencies. Commendable programs such as NSF's IGERT program do exist, but much more is needed.[169]

Many of the basic skills of entrepreneurship and technology transfer can be taught. Some students display an aptitude for entrepreneurship; their talents can be fostered and developed. Universities should see these tasks as a part of their educational responsibility. We give some examples of activities and programs along these lines.

Many large universities now have an annual business plan competition.[170] Such competitions have often become the central catalyst in training students to be entrepreneurs. They attract both graduate and undergraduate students, teaming up engineering and business school students, and often matching up students with experienced entrepreneurs from the community as well as students from neighboring universities. The competitions make use of a full ecosystem of world-class entrepreneurs, investors, and potential partners, courses on business plan creation, feedback on business models from judging panels, and team-building skill development.

Forbes recently highlighted MIT's $100K Entrepreneurship Competition (begun in 1989), as well as competitions at Rice University, the Venture Labs Investment Competition at University of Texas at Austin, Harvard University, the Wharton School of Business at the University of Pennsylvania, the University of California at Berkeley, the Duke University Startup Challenge, the Dartmouth Entrepreneurial Network, the McGinnis Venture Competition at Carnegie Mellon University, New York University (NYU), the University of Chicago, the University of Oregon, Tufts University, and Purdue University.[171]

Many universities also have entrepreneurship centers. At the University of Southern California (USC) Stevens Institute for Innovation, a team of 30 professionals helps faculty and students throughout USC's professional schools and undergraduate college develop their ideas for start-ups, nonprofits, new products, or licenses and helps them acquire skills for lifelong innovation. USC's Stevens Institute also provides a central connection for industrial partners seeking cutting-edge innovations in which to invest. MIT's Entrepreneurship Center (E-center) fosters entrepreneurial activities in education and research, alliances, and across the overall community.

Entrepreneurship centers like these are different from traditional technology licensing offices (discussed below). They are more closely tied to the university's educational mission and may report to an academic provost rather than to a vice president for research.

Also noteworthy are programs at the junction between engineering and business schools, such as the new Master of Entrepreneurship program at the University of Michigan, offered jointly by the School of Business and the College of Engineering.[172]

Prepare Students for National and Grand Challenges

The United States and indeed the world as a whole face a number of pressing "grand challenges," including energy, water, climate, food supply, and biodiversity. The challenges require researchers to understand and investigate complex systems, such as the evolution and threat assessment of severe storms and the next-generation grid for energy transmission, that involve not just fundamental scientific and technical concepts, including high-performance computation, but also economics, human behavior, and policy. To prepare students to deal with such issues, universities need to go beyond training within traditional disciplines and to institute or expand the scope of project-based, multidisciplinary learning.

These grand challenges, moreover, tend to attract a different, and sometimes more diverse, population of students than those who see themselves as future entrepreneurs in the private sector. While the prospect of founding new companies is inspiring to some students, others may be inspired by the idealism of doing well in the world. These goals are not incompatible. Universities need both kinds of students—in addition, of course, to those who will be motivated simply by the search for new knowledge.

Provide More Undergraduate Research Experiences

The typical model of undergraduate education has long been the acquisition of basic knowledge, both for personal enrichment and as a foundation for developing critical analytical skills. These skills prepare students for employment or for further education. Research leading to the creation of new knowledge has traditionally been deferred until graduate school. This tradition is changing, however, as more universities are actively encouraging undergraduate students to participate in authentic research.

There are compelling reasons to add a research component to undergraduate education. First, there is abundant anecdotal evidence that an interesting summer job or other extramural opportunity can inspire students to pursue further study in science, technology, engineering, and mathematics. Personally experiencing the thrill of discovery widens a student's perspective on possible careers in basic or applied fields.

In addition, research experience hones broadly valuable attributes such as tractable problem definition and hypothesis testing, as well as critical intangibles like creativity, determination, and perseverance. Students may work closely with a senior research mentor or as part of a team; both models yield great benefits. A recent PCAST report gives quantitative details on the critical workforce need for STEM-qualified personnel and the importance of early research experiences as a strategy to meet that need.[173]

Many universities are promoting undergraduate research experiences. The University of Texas at Austin's Freshman Research Initiative places more than 500 students every year, with the goal of eventually reaching all entering freshmen in the natural sciences.[174] The University of Michigan recruits faculty and research scientists to sponsor undergraduate research projects and helps undergraduates find an exciting project and a research mentor.[175] Universities are raising modest funds for these projects from alumni. The number of research opportunities available remains small, however, because undergraduate research commands only limited support in the Federal R&D budget. For example, funding for NSF's Research Experiences for Undergraduates (REU) program, the largest such program in any agency, is $67 million per year, about 1 percent of the NSF budget.[176] REU supports about 9,000 students, mostly in summer research programs. Expanding undergraduate research opportunities could offer an excellent opportunity for greater numbers of students to connect with the private sector, improving the relationship between educational institutions and industry and, for a modest investment, increasing the supply of skilled workers to the private sector. The infrastructure and the mentors already exist, but more funding is needed. In addition, universities need to restructure traditional undergraduate teaching labs to adapt them to discovery-based research courses.

6.3. Increasing and Deepening Interactions with Industry

Action #5.3. Embrace more fully the additional role of universities as hubs of the innovation ecosystem.

Federal support of basic and applied research provides universities and industry with a foundational platform for the development of ideas and technologies with commercial potential. As described in Section 3.4, the ability of universities and industry to make use of this platform was transformed in 1980, when the Bayh-Dole Act gave intellectual-property control to universities for inventions made by their employees working on Government-funded research. Up until 1980, the Government had accumulated 28,000 patents, but fewer than 5 percent were licensed to industry for development of products.[177] Since 1980, universities have been responsible for bringing commercial ideas and technologies to the marketplace, giving them a critical place in the innovation ecosystem. A 2002 editorial in the *Economist Technology Quarterly* summed up the benefits of Bayh-Dole:[178]

> Possibly the most inspired piece of legislation to be enacted in America over the past half-century was the Bayh-Dole act of 1980. Together with amendments in 1984 and augmentation in 1986, this unlocked all the inventions and discoveries that had been made in laboratories throughout the United States with the help of taxpayers' money. More than anything, this single policy measure helped to reverse America's precipitous slide into industrial irrelevance. Since 1980, American universities have witnessed a tenfold increase in the patents they generate, spun off more than 2,200 firms to exploit research done in their labs, created 260,000 jobs in the process, and now contribute $40 billion annually to the American economy.

Technology Licensing and Technology Startups

In the 30 years since Bayh-Dole, universities have developed a wide range of technology licensing offices (TLOs). Intellectual property (IP) and its licensing is one of the major concerns of Chief Technology Officers in industry regarding their relationships with universities. Some universities have very flexible policies; others are less so. Some TLOs are supported through university core funding and can afford to be ambitious in pursuing and marketing patents. Others operate solely on the income from patent licensing and are more constrained in the number of patents they can develop.

Although it is appropriate for IP income to defray the cost of technology-transfer operations, it is unwise for patenting and licensing policies and practices to have the sole purpose of maximizing income to the university. A report by the National Research Council on IP management at universities made this point as its first finding: "The first goal of university technology transfer involving IP is the expeditious and wide dissemination of university-generated technology for the public good."[179] The University of Michigan, as one example, orders its goals: "to facilitate the efficient transfer of knowledge and technology from the University to the private sector in support of the public interest; to support the discovery of new knowledge and technology; [and] to attract resources for the support of University programs…."[180]

Additional goals of TLOs include supporting the faculty researchers who integrate innovation into the academic environment and protecting the use of new technology for further academic research. Many universities have refined their practices to set a priority on helping original investigators start new companies, even when that means losing potential short-term cash revenue from licensing their IP to larger companies. Others have developed internal sharing models between the TLO, researchers, and their departments and have devised simple and transparent mechanisms for transfer.

Among the novel programs are the University of Minnesota's "innovation partnerships," wherein a company sponsoring research at the university is able to prepay a fee and receive an exclusive worldwide license, with royalties taking effect only in cases of significant commercial success.[181] Penn State University has taken the dramatic step of no longer mandating university ownership of intellectual property associated with industry-funded research, believing that the greater value is not in IP ownership, but rather in increased student and faculty contact with the real problems that industry (under this favorable model) will bring. Penn State's Vice President of Research, Henry Foley, has said, "We're moving to the position where if a corporation sponsors research with us, they own it. We prefer ... to get the interactions, the relationships and the ability to work on more pressing problems."[182]

Technology licensing should be flexible enough to accommodate both small start-ups (which obtain license rights in exchange for equity, since they are typically capital-poor) and large companies (which pay cash royalties in the traditional way). Statistics from the Association of University Technology Managers (AUTM) show that most start-up deals with universities involve some equity exchange.[183] Stanford has had a particularly rich tradition of licensing to the technology creators for equity. To date, it has received income of $336 million from Google alone.[184]

Today, most universities record only the number of transfers and the profit or loss of their TLOs. Broader metrics are needed to fully capture the value of the technology-transfer ecosystem. The America COMPETES Act[185] provides that the NSF should work with the National Academy of Sciences to evaluate, develop, and create a set of metrics for measuring the impact of research on society. This collaboration could be expanded to include a set of influential university TLOs, so that the resulting metrics can be used consistently by the NSF and TLOs throughout the university system.

Proof-of-Concept Centers and Other Translational Platforms

Chapter 3 describes the proof-of-concept centers (POCCs) of several research universities at the forefront of innovation. We commend the POCC model for broader adoption. POCCs select some of a university's best ideas for commercialization and typically over a 2-to 4-year cycle put these ideas and their associated teams through peer review, find industry mentorship, and provide small commercial grants to help transition the innovation into a market-ready start-up. The POCC's essential role is to reduce technology and market risk to the point where an external investor will decide it is worth making the investment to further commercialize (i.e. productize) the technology.

We endorse recent Government efforts to expand POCCs and related translational platforms. In July 2011, the NSF formed and announced a national Innovation Corps (I-Corps) to provide mentoring and seed funds for individual scientific efforts in universities without POCCs. The first grants, sized around $50,000, were announced in October 2011. Grantees must have an active NSF award or one that has been active within the previous 5 years. The I-Corps hopes to fund about 25 new opportunities each quarter; however, this is less than 1 percent of the 12,000 grants made annually by the NSF. While I-Corps cannot afford to fund a local POCC on all of the campuses it supports, it is dedicated to creating a nationwide community of I-Corps mentors. NIH's recent creation of a new national institute, the National Center for Advancing Translational Sciences (NCATS), also shows welcome new recognition of the need for new translational platforms.[186]

Many universities have not yet created POCCs but conduct proof-of-concept review sessions allowing academics and investors to evaluate ideas together. At the University of Virginia, for example, such review sessions have led to several $100,000 seed grants from external foundations. These review sessions, which can also be good feeders into the I-Corps system, are excellent forerunners to the creation of POCCs.

In 2011, in the i6 Green program, the U.S. Commerce Department Economic Development Administration distributed $12 million from various U.S. agencies among several new POCCs dedicated to clean-energy-technology innovation. The POCCs chosen included those at Louisiana Tech University, the University of Florida, the University of Iowa, Michigan State University, a New England regional consortium, and Washington State University. Universities have been particularly prolific in creating commercial opportunities in clean technology and energy. In a recent presentation, Ray Rothrock, Managing Director at the venture capital firm Venrock and incoming chair of the National Venture Capital Association (NVCA), reported a survey finding that 32 percent of the initial-round clean-tech venture investments went to start-ups spawned from universities.

POCCs have proven to be key in facilitating commercialization efforts that fill in the funding gap between research and new company incorporation. The small amounts of money they provide offer huge end-stage leverage for the billions of dollars of research money already spent; university research by itself does not passively spill over into commercialization and innovation. POCC funds also provide huge initial leverage against the millions of dollars of investment money that will follow once a company incorporates; these investments rely on a thorough understanding of technology and product fit to market need. The creation of POCCs has shined light on the nature of commercialization, and whether universities have formal POCCS or not, many have reviewed their technology licensing structures to make sure that they help, not hinder, innovation and commercialization.

The biggest challenge for POCCs is their lack of a revenue model beyond the generosity of donors. It is difficult to ask entrepreneurs to donate stock to a POCC when they will also be required to allocate stock to the TLO at the time of incorporation. Based on current models, POCCs cost from $1 million to $3 million a year for operating expenses and grants, but their leverage can be large. We recommend that universities pursue public-private partnerships, including state and philanthropic funding, to create and maintain their POCCs.

Leadership in Establishing New Public-Private Partnerships

Universities should take a stronger leadership role in proposing, initiating, hosting, and participating in public-private partnerships (PPPs). PPPs are an appropriate mechanism when two conditions are met: a critical national interest is stake (e.g., in energy, health, or national security), and there are barriers to innovation that private sector companies working alone cannot overcome. If the Government is a major purchaser or regulator of the sector's output (e.g., in medical products or some energy applications), then Government participation through a PPP has additional benefits in the early stages of R&D—early guidance on Government needs can avert wasted effort. Universities, as neutral third parties and hubs of early applied research, are uniquely positioned to identify and promote new PPPs meeting these criteria. Proposals with a substantial and demonstrable university pedigree are also less open to attack from those who criticize Government attempts to pick winners and losers.

The United States established a flagship PPP, SEMATECH, in the 1980s, to accelerate innovation in the U.S. semiconductor industry. More recently, however, other countries have supported PPPs on a much larger scale than the United States. For example, in 2007, the European Commission and the European Federation of Pharmaceutical Industries and Associations (EFPIA) launched the Innovative Medicine Initiative, with funding of €2 billion (coming equally from industry and government) spread over two dozen participating companies. Other overseas examples include Germany's Fraunhofer Institutes, Singapore's Venture Acceleration Centre, Taiwan's NSC Science and Technology Parks, and the Zhongguancun Science Park ("China's Silicon Valley") in Beijing, the home of Lenovo.[187]

PPPs in the United States have long been supported through mechanisms such as the Small Business Innovation Research (SBIR) program and Federal technology-transfer processes but have not reached the level of funding of the prominent foreign examples previously cited. NIH's recent establishment of a new National Center for Advancing Translational Sciences (NCATS), whose programs involve a national consortium of medical research institutions,[188] is a positive step. We consider public-private partnerships a ripe area for further investment, especially with university participation and leadership.

6.4. Engaging on National Workforce Issues

Action #5.4. Confront difficult career-development and workforce issues, including length of time to Ph.D. and the reliance of the S&T enterprise on the labor of early career training positions.

The United States is the world leader in basic research, performed at universities, Federal laboratories, and independent research institutes; led by principal investigators, university faculty, and laboratory staff; and populated by graduate students, postdoctoral researchers, and other research staff. The high standing of U.S. universities, research institutes, and laboratories derives both from the quality of the graduate programs (i.e., the training of students as researchers) and from the quality and volume of research results, measured by publications in leading journals, citations, patents, etc.

Indeed, the research enterprise depends on the relatively inexpensive labor provided by students and post-doctoral scholars. These early career scientists are a crucial part of the U.S. research enterprise. This dependence creates a potential conflict between the need to maintain the size of this early career workforce and the need to advance the careers of the talented researchers who will keep the American research ecosystem the most productive in the world. While compensation should reflect the nature of junior positions as researchers in training, the issues of graduate student and postdoctoral researcher numbers and the duration of doctoral programs and postdoctoral appointments are serious ones that need to reflect realistic expectations for future career opportunities. We need to be training people for science and engineering jobs that are likely to exist, for example in the private sector, and less for jobs that will be more scarce, assuming no significant increase in university tenured faculty.[189]

Universities need to take a stronger role in managing the time that graduate students take to get their degrees. Overly long times to degree are costly, waste precious graduate education resources, and serve as a disincentive for attracting bright minds to STEM fields. Several reports over the last decade have documented the long time interval needed for degree completion.[190] The best data comes from the NSF's Survey of Earned Doctorates, although the most recent data are from 2003.[191] The median total years spent in graduate school, less reported periods of non-enrollment, was 6.9 for the life sciences, 6.8 for the physical sciences, and 6.9 for engineering. This is too much time. While the last decade has seen some progress on the issue, in many fields, times to degree in absolute terms remain too long.[192] There is no evidence that the quality of the graduate education is higher in those departments in which the time to degree is longer. University administrations need to take a critical look at the time to degree for Ph.Ds. when reviewing a department's performance.

The growing number of post-doctoral scholars and the length of time spent in postdoctoral positions, most notably in the life sciences, must likewise be confronted. A recent NRC report documents that the number of biomedical Ph.Ds. increased from 5500 per year in the period 1997-2003 to 7100 in 2008, a 30 percent increase in 6 years.[193] Over the same period the number of tenure and tenure-track faculty positions has been constant at about 30,000, and there is no reported prospect of significant expansion in the foreseeable future.

While academic positions are the dominant employment for biomedical researchers immediately after completion of a Ph.D. (the post-doctoral fellowship years),[194] beginning 6 years after the completion of a Ph.D. in biomedical research, non-academic positions employ the majority rather than academic positions (including tenured, tenure-track, and staff positions).[195]

It thus seems that a significant fraction of today's postdoctoral fellows in biomedical research are essentially in training for jobs that do not exist in academia or for jobs in industry of other sectors into which they could move sooner. They are, de facto, low-paid university research staff. During the period in which the NIH budget doubled in real terms, postdoctoral salaries barely increased to keep pace with inflation. A decade-old recommendation of the National Research Council that the NIH increase post-doctoral salaries substantially has largely not happened.[196] Recent increases in NIH's NRSA postdoctoral fellowship stipends, of which about 3000 are awarded annually, have amounted to less than the concurrent inflation rate and have not reversed the previous erosion in compensation.[197] We see no long-term satisfactory equilibrium unless universities, or their funding agencies, limit the number of postdoctoral researchers to be consistent with feasible career advancement to faculty or private-sector positions. A replacement system, better matched to the increased role of the universities in the innovation system, is an expansion of non-faculty career research and research management positions. These may be short-term or long-term as university resources and sources of funding may dictate, but they should be career, not training, positions. In short, there is a mismatch between the large number of Federally supported postdocs and graduate students who per-form much of the biomedical research at universities and the opportunities and needs of the non-university workforce.

How to fix the biomedical workforce mismatch while preserving the research enterprise is a complex and challenging problem. Universities can contribute to a solution by more aggressively managing the duration of biomedical Ph.D. programs and the number of biomedical post-doctoral researchers employed. They can adopt and enforce policies that are consistent with realistic career expectations for the individuals involved. Such management may reduce the biomedical graduate student and postdoctoral populations at some institutions, and it might shrink the number of graduate programs. But future job needs in industry, at National Laboratories, or in broader career sectors will be better served by shorter, more efficient, programs, along with a measured expansion of non-faculty career opportunities at universities and broader educational opportunities for graduate students as discussed in Section 6.2.

For the physical sciences, the problem is smaller, but similar in kind. In 2009 the majority (52.3 percent) of Ph.Ds. in the physical sciences was found in industry and business, and the clear majority (72.7 percent) of engineering Ph.Ds. was found in industry.[198] These students would benefit from many of the policies PCAST suggested here for the biomedical disciplines. In particular, as they are largely industry bound, these students, as well as the entire research eco-system, would profit from the educational modernization suggested in Section 6.2.

A final point relating to the science and technology workforce is worth emphasizing: The U.S. research enterprise needs all the talent, skills, and brainpower that it can get. In fields where women are underrepresented, and in the even greater number of fields where there is significant underrepresentation by minorities, continuing efforts at reducing barriers are needed. Universities must continue to be central in such efforts.

VII. Summary of Recommendations

7.1. Opportunities and Actions Recommended in This Report

Key Opportunity #1. The Nation has the opportunity to maintain its world-leading position in research investment, structured as a mutually supporting partnership among industry, the Federal Government, universities, and other governmental and private entities.

Action #1.1. PCAST recommends reaffirming the President's goal that total R&D expenditures should achieve and sustain a level of 3 percent of GDP. Congressional authorization committees should take ownership of pieces of that goal, with the Executive Branch and Congress establishing policies to enhance private industry's major share. (Section 4.1)

Action #1.2. Recognizing its political difficulty, PCAST nevertheless urges Congress and the Executive Branch to find one or more mechanisms for increasing the stability and predictability of Federal research funding, including funding for research infrastructure and facilities. Possibilities include a cross-agency multiyear program and financial plan akin to DoD's Future Years Defense Program (FYDP) or a closer coupling of multiyear authorizations to actual appropriations for R&D. (Section 4.1)

Action #1.3. The Research and Experimentation Tax Credit (usually called the R&D tax credit) needs to be made permanent. An increase in the rate of the alternative simplified credit from 14 percent to 20 percent would not be excessive. The credit also needs to be made more useful to small and medium enterprises that are R&D intensive by instituting any or all of (1) refundable tax credits, (2) transferable tax credits, or (3) modifications in the definition of net operating loss to give advantage to R&D expenditures. (Section 4.2)

Action #1.4. The Federal Government should adopt policies that increase the productivity of researchers, including more people-based awards, larger and longer awards for some merit-selected investigators, and administratively efficient grant mechanisms. (Section 4.3)

Key Opportunity #2. The Federal Government has the opportunity to enhance its role as the enduring foundational investor in basic and early applied research in the United States. It can adopt policies that are most consistent with that role. Federal policy can seek to foster a sustainable R&D enterprise in which, when research is deemed worth supporting, it is supported for success.

Action #2.1. The Federal Government should identify and achieve regulatory policy reforms, particularly relating to the regulatory burdens on research universities. (Section 4.4)

- PCAST concurs with the substance of the AAU-APLU-COGR consensus list.

Action #2.2. The Federal agencies should appropriately circumscribe the use of cost sharing. (Section 4.4)

- Apply 2009 NSF cost-sharing reforms Government-wide.

Key Opportunity #3. Federal agencies have the opportunity to grow portfolios that more strategically support a mix of evolutionary vs. revolutionary research, disciplinary vs. inter-disciplinary work, and project-based vs. people-based awards.

Action #3.1. Each agency should have a strategic plan that explicitly addresses the different kinds of research activities that can contribute to its mission, specifically addressing the axes of evolutionary vs. revolutionary research, disciplinary vs. interdisciplinary work, and project-based vs. people-based awards. (Section 4.5)

Action #3.2. Each agency should diversify its mechanisms for merit review to be optimal for the portfolio in its strategic plan. (Section 4.5)

Action #3.3. Each agency should adopt policies that increase the agility of funding new fields, unexpected opportunities, and the creativity of new researchers. (Section 4.5)

- Increase funding for fellowships (including portable) and training grants.
- Fund more early-career opportunities.

Key Opportunity #4. There is the opportunity for the Government to create additional policy encouragements and incentives for industry to invest in research, both on its own and in new partnerships with universities and National Laboratories.

Action #4.1. Improve STEM education so as to produce more and better home-grown researchers and technology entrepreneurs. (Section 5.1)

- Two previous PCAST reports on STEM education recommend policy directions.

Action #4.2. Attract and retain, both for universities and industry, the world's best researchers and students from abroad. (Section 5.1)

- Visa reform for high-ability STEM graduates.

Action #4.3. Support the President's Export Control Reform Initiative and further measures. (Section 5.2)

- Reduce "deemed export" burdens on universities.
- Unleash U.S. firms to compete internationally.

Action #4.4. Enable streamlined interactions between U.S. National Laboratories and industry. (Section 5.3)

- Actions needed by both laboratory leadership and sponsoring agencies

Key Opportunity #5. Research universities have the opportunity to strengthen and enhance their additional role as hubs of the innovation ecosystem. While maintaining the intellectual depth of their foundations in basic research, they can change their educational programs to better prepare their graduates to work in today's world. They can become more proactive in transferring research results into the private sector.

Action #5.1. Maintain strong commitment to the scope and intellectual depth of fundamental university research. (Section 6.1)

- Fundamental research provides the foundation for world-changing new industries.

Action #5.2. Augment the educational mission to today's world. (Section 6.2)

- Train for entrepreneurship and technology transfer.
- Prepare for national needs and grand challenges.
- Increase undergraduate research experiences.

Action #5.3. Embrace more fully the additional role of universities as hubs of the innovation ecosystem. (Section 6.3)

- Technology licensing best practices.
- Proof of concept centers.
- Leadership in public-private partnerships.

Action #5.4. Confront difficult career-development and workforce issues, including length of time to Ph.D. and the reliance of the S&T enterprise on the labor of early-career training positions. (Section 6.4)

7.2. Relationship to Other Recent Report Recommendations

Many of the actions that we recommend here reiterate recommendations of other recent PCAST reports in specific disciplines such as energy, nanotechnology, information technology, advanced manufacturing, ecosystems, and two reports on improving STEM education.[199] This report thus serves to highlight the crosscutting nature of many recommended actions and their importance for the entire science and technology enterprise. Some examples follow.

From PCAST's advanced manufacturing report:

- Extend the R&D tax credit permanently and increase the rate to 17 percent, as advocated in the Presidents' Strategy for American Innovation and FY2012 budget request. Knowing that the credit will persist will encourage firms to lengthen their time horizon for R&D investments. The rules governing the tax credit should also be examined to make clear that R&D on manufacturing processes qualifies for the credit.
- Use Federal policy and leadership to fulfill the President's goal that public and private investment R&D reach 3 percent of GDP.
- Expand the number of high-skilled foreign workers that may be employed by U.S. companies. This can be done by such policies as allowing foreign students that receive a graduate degree in STEM from a U.S. university to receive a green card, allowing each employment-based visa to automatically cover a worker and his or her spouse and children, and increasing the number of H-1B visas.

From PCAST's energy technologies report:

- DOE should establish a training grant program at universities similar to the NIH and NSF training grant programs. These programs would address critical energy workforce needs in such areas as power electronics, energy storage, radionuclide chemistry, and combustion, and the related areas of IT, social sciences, etc. These would support not only graduate students but also curriculum development, postdoctoral researchers, integrated departmental programs, and undergraduate support.

From PCAST's "Engage to Excel" STEM report:

- Catalyze widespread adoption of empirically validated teaching practices.
- Advocate and provide support for replacing standard laboratory courses with discovery-based research courses.

- Encourage partnerships among stakeholders to diversify pathways to STEM careers.

Similarly, many of our recommendations resonate affirmatively with those of recent important studies by organizations outside of Government. Indeed, where these reports provide detailed factual and statistical support for recommendations in common, we have often not repeated such material in this report. Here are a few examples of significant concurrence (by no means intended as full summaries of the indicated reports):

From the American Academy of Arts and Science's 2008 *Advancing Research in Science and Engineering* (*ARISE*):[200]

- Create or strengthen existing large, multiyear awards for early career faculty.
- Provide seed funding for early career faculty to enable them to explore new ideas for which no results have yet been achieved.
- Consider targeted programs, grant mechanisms, and policies—and adapt existing grant programs—to foster transformative research; establish metrics with which to evaluate their success.
- Strengthen the application and review processes. High-risk research proposals face even greater challenges in a stressed peer-review system not equipped to appreciate them.
- Establish new research programs only if they have enough critical mass to avoid fruitless grant-writing efforts. Grant programs that fund a very small percentage of applications are inefficient uses of money, time, and effort.

From the National Research Council's 2012 Research Universities and the Future of America:[201]

- The Federal Government should review and modify those research policies and practices governing university research and graduate education that have become burden-some and inefficient, such as research cost reimbursement, unnecessary regulation, and awkward variation and coordination among Federal agencies.
- As a core component of a national plan to raise total national R&D funded by all sources to 3 percent of GDP, Congress and the Administration should provide full funding of the amount authorized by the America COMPETES Act, which would double the level of

basic research conducted by NSF, NIST, and DOE Science, as well as sustain the Nation's investment in other key areas of basic research, including biomedical research. Within this investment, as recommended by *Rising Above the Gathering Storm*, a portion of the increase should be directed to high-risk, innovative, and unconventional research.

- The relationship between business and higher education should evolve into more of a peer-to-peer nature, stressing collaboration in areas of joint interest rather than the traditional customer-supplier relationship in which business procures graduates and intellectual property from universities.
- Within the context of also making the R&D tax credit permanent, implement new tax policies that incentivize business to develop partnerships with universities (and others as warranted) for research that results in new U.S.-located economic activities.
- Collaboration among the National Laboratories, business, and universities should also be encouraged, since the university's capacity for large-scale, sustained research projects both supports and depends critically on both the participation of university faculty and graduate students as well as the marketplace.

From the 2012 Report of the Biomedical Research Workforce working group of the NIH Advisory Committee to the Director:[202]

- To ensure that all graduate students supported by the NIH receive excellent training, NIH should increase the proportion of graduate students supported by training grants and fellowships compared with those supported by research project grants, without increasing the overall number of graduate student positions.
- NIH should create a program to supplement training grants through competitive review to allow institutions to provide additional training and career-development experiences to equip students for various career options, and it should test ways to shorten the Ph.D. training period.
- NIH should revise the peer-review criteria for training grants to include consideration of outcomes of all students in the relevant Ph.D. programs at those institutions, not only those supported by the training grant. Study sections reviewing graduate training programs should be

educated to value a range of career outcomes. This recommendation could be phased in relatively quickly.

- To encourage timely completion of graduate degrees, NIH should cap the number of years a graduate student can be supported by NIH funds (any combination of training grants, fellowships, and research project grants), with an institutional average of 5 years, and no one individual allowed to receive support for more than 6 years…NIH should continue to assess the pre-doctoral stipend level annually.

From the National Science Board's commentary on Science and Engineering Indicators 2012:[203]

- Basic and applied R&D that the private sector is unlikely to support sufficiently requires sustained, direct funding by the Federal Government to create a knowledge base of potentially transformative ideas that are critical building blocks of innovation.
- Federally funded academic R&D is instrumental in creating and sustaining a world-class higher education system that prepares the next generation of American scientists and engineers and also attracts and trains high-ability international students, researchers, and faculty.
- Appropriate visa policies enable the attraction and retention of the best and brightest foreign-born students, faculty, researchers, and S&E workers.

From AAU/APLU/COGR's Recommendations to the National Research Council on Regulatory and Financial Reform of Federal Research Policy:[204]

- Prohibit voluntary committed cost sharing across the Federal Government and create a mandatory cost-sharing exemption for research universities.
- Harmonize regulations and information systems between agencies and statutes where reasonable and eliminate unnecessary duplication and redundancy.
- Eliminate regulations that do not add value or enhance accountability. At least two requirements, Effort Reporting and Cost Accounting Standards, neither add value nor enhance accountability.
- Reinforce the original intent of the Single Audit Act.

From Business Roundtable's 2012 report *Action for America*:[205]

- Create a new STEM green card for foreign students who graduate from U.S. universities with advanced degrees in STEM fields.
- Increase the standard H-1B visa cap and remove the cap for advanced degree holders so that all foreign nationals who receive a master's degree or higher from a U.S. university can be eligible for an H-1B visa.
- Make every feature of the reformed U.S. corporate tax code permanent, establishing the high-priority objective of eliminating corporate tax policy uncertainty.

The number and concordance of multiple studies, some with a congressional charter, by deliberative academies, university and industry advocacy groups, and others indicate a strong national consensus on actions that are needed now.

PCAST Future of the U.S. Science and Technology Research Enterprise Working Group

Working Group members participated in the preparation of an initial draft of this report.

Those working group members who are not PCAST members are not responsible for, nor necessarily endorse, the final version of this report as modified and approved by PCAST.

Co-Chairs

William Press*
Raymer Professor in Computer Science and Integrative Biology
University of Texas at Austin

Maxine Savitz*
Vice President
National Academy of Engineering

* Denotes PCAST Member.

Members

Safi R. Bahcall
President and Chief Executive Officer
Synta Pharma

Rosina Bierbaum[*]
Professor of Natural Resources and Environmental Policy
School of Natural Resources and Environment and School of Public Health University of Michigan

Jean-Lou Chameau
President
California Institute of Technology

S. James Gates, Jr.[*]
John S. Toll Professor of Physics
Director, Center for String and Particle Theory
University of Maryland, College Park

Mark Gorenberg[*]
Managing Director
Hummer Winblad Venture Partners

Eric Schmidt[*]
Chief Executive
Google, Inc.

Thomas Hunter
President and Laboratories Director (retired)
Sandia Corporation

Eric Lander[*]
President
Broad Institute of Harvard and MIT

Chad Mirkin[*]
Rathmann Professor, Chemistry, Materials Science and Engineering, Chemical and Biological Engineering and Medicine
Director, International Institute for Nanotechnology
Northwestern University

Ernest J. Moniz[*]
Cecil and Ida Green Professor of Physics and Engineering Systems
Director, MIT's Initiative
Massachusetts Institute of Technology

Michael Witherell
Vice Chancellor for Research
University of California Presidential Chair, Physics Department
University of California, Santa Barbara

[*] Denotes PCAST Member.

Daniel Schrag* Sturgis Hooper Professor of Geology Professor, Environmental Science and Engineering
Director, Harvard University Center for Environment
Harvard University

Maria T. Zuber
Chair, Department of Earth, Atmospheric, and Planetary Science
E. A. Griswold Professor of Geophysics
Massachusetts Institute of Technology

Staff

Danielle Evers†
AAAS Science and Technology Policy Fellow

Amber Hartman Scholz
Assistant Executive Director, PCAST

APPENDIX A. EXPERTS CONSULTED

PCAST is grateful for the input of the following individual experts. Listing here does not imply endorsement of this report or its recommendations.

Peter Agre
Professor, Johns Hopkins Bloomberg School of Public Health

May Berenbaum
Professor and Department Head, Department of Entomology, University of Illinois at Urbana-Champaign

Sylvia Ceyer
Head of the Department of Chemistry and J.C. Sheehan Professor of Chemistry,

Regina Dugan‡
Director, Defense Advanced Research Projects Agency (DARPA)

David Eisenbud
Vice President for Mathematics and the Physical Sciences, Simons Foundation Professor of Mathematics
University of California at Berkeley

Kaigham J. Gabriel*
Deputy Director, Defense Advanced Research Projects Agency (DARPA)

† PCAST staff member until June 2012.

‡ Regina Dugan left her role as Director of DARPA in March 2012. She now serves as a senior executive at Google, Inc.

* Ken Gabriel has served as Acting Director of DARPA since March 2012.

Massachusetts Institute of Technology

Rita Colwell
Distinguished University Professor, University of Maryland at College Park and Johns Hopkins University Bloomberg School of Public Health; Chairman Emeritus and Senior Advisor, Canon U.S. Life Sciences, Inc.; President, CosmosID, Inc.

David Goldston
Director of Government Affairs, Natural Resources Defense Council

Robert Conn
President, Kavli Foundation

Bart Gordon
Partner, K&L Gates; Distinguished Fellow, Council of Competitiveness
Former U.S. Representative from Tennessee
Former Chairman, House Committee on Science and Technology

Persis Drell
Professor and Director, SLAC National Accelerator Laboratory

Congressman Rush Holt
U.S. Representative from New District

A.G. Lafely
Former Chairman of the Board, President, and CEO, Procter and Gamble

Alfred Spector
Vice President of Strategy and Technology,
Google; CTO, IBM Software Business

Peter Lee
Distinguished Scientist and Managing Director, Microsoft Research

Craig B. Thompson
President and Chief Executive Officer, Memorial Sloan-Kettering Cancer Center (MSKCC)

Alan Leshner
Chief Executive Officer, American Association for the Advancement Science; Executive Publisher, *Science*

Hai Tran
Policy Analyst, Office of Management and Budget

John C. Mather
Senior Project Scientist, James Webb Space Telescope, Goddard Space Flight Center

Michael Turner
Rauner Distinguished Service Professor and Director, Kavli Institute for Cosmological Physics, The University of Chicago

Franklin M. ("Lynn") Orr, Jr.
Director, Precourt Institute for Energy; Keleen & Carlton Beal Professor, Stanford University

Jeffrey Wadsworth
President and Chief Executive Officer, Battelle Memorial Institute

Michael Rosenblatt
Executive Vice President and Chief Medical Officer, Merck & Co., Inc.

William Wulf
AT&T Professor of Computer Science and University Professor, University of Virginia

Randy Schekman
Professor, Department of Molecular and Cell Biology, University of California, Berkeley; Investigator, Howard Hughes Medical Institute

End Notes

[1] Vannevar Bush, "Science—The Endless Frontier, A Report to the President," July 1945, www.nsf.gov/od/lpa/nsf50/vbush1945.htm

[2] Roger Pielke ("In Retrospect: Science—The Endless Frontier," *Nature*, 19 August 2010, Vol. 466, p. 922) discusses historical swings in the meaning and use of the term "basic research" and related words (not always with the same meaning) such as "fundamental," and "transformational." Our use of the terms "basic" and "applied" is compatible with those of the Federal Government (see NSF, "Definitions of Research and Development: An Annotated Compilation of Official Sources" at http://www.nsf.gov/statistics. We distinguish early applied research from later applied research to make explicit that "applied" research includes much that is pre-commercial.

[3] *Science* derives from the Latin terms *scientia*, from *sciens* "having knowledge," from *scire* "to know," www.merriam-webster.com/dictionary/science

[4] CRS Report for Congress, "Life Expectancy in the United States," Order Code RL32792, updated August 16, 2006.

[5] R. Schimerling, "Harvard Health Publications," Harvard Medical School, 2009.

[6] Jon Cohen, "HIV as Treatment as Prevention," *Science*, 23 Dec 2011, Vol. 334, No. 6063, p. 1628.

[7] David E. Bloom and David Canning, "Health and Economic Growth: Reconciling the Micro and Macro Evidence," Number 42, *CDDRL Working Papers*, 2005, iis-db.stanford.edu/pubs/20924/BloomCanning_42.pdf

[8] "Secretary Clinton's Remarks at the Global Philanthropy Forum Conference," April 22, 2009, at www.state

[9] National Hurricane Center, "NHC Tropical Cyclone Forecast Verification," at www.nhc.noaa.gov/verification/verify5.shtml

[10] T. Dyson, "World Food Trends and Prospects," *Proc. Nat. Acad. Sci.*, 96, 5929-5936, 1999.

[11] M.L. Parry, O.F. Canziani, J.P. Palutikof, P.J. van der Linden, and C.E. Hanson (eds), "Contribution of Working Group II to the Fourth Assessment Report of the Intergovernmental Panel on Climate Change," 2007 at ipcc.ch/publications_and_data/ar4/wg2/en/contents.html

[12] U.S. Environmental Protection Agency. Clean Watershed Needs Survey 2008: Report to Congress. EPA-832-R-10-002, at water

[13] Keith Devlin, *Mathematics: The New Golden Age* (New York: Columbia University Press, 1999).

[14] "Particle Accelerators Help Develop New Cancer Fighting Drug," *Symmetry Breaking*, August 26, 2011. www.symmetrymagazine.org/breaking/2011/08/26/particle-accelerators-helps-develop-new-cancer

[15] G. Washington, "First Annual Message to Congress," January 8, 1790, www.pbs.org/georgewashington/collection/other_1790jan8.html

[16] Pew Research Center for the People and The Press. "Public Praises Science; Scientists Fault Public, Media: Scientific Achievements Less Prominent Than a Decade Ago," July 9, 2009, people-press.org/2009/07/09/public-praises-science

[17] R. M. Solow, "Technical Change and the Aggregate Production Function," *Review of Economics and Statistics*, 39: 312–320, 1957.

[18] NESTA, *The Innovation Index: Measuring the UK's Investment in Innovation and Its Effects* (London: NESTA, 2009, 4), www.nesta.org.uk/library/documents/innovation-index.pdf

[19] Robert Atkinson and Luke Stewart, "University Research Funding: The United States is Behind and Falling," 2011; The Information Technology and Innovation Foundation (ITIF); Committee on Prospering in the Global Economy of the 21st Century: An Agenda for American Science and Technology, National Academy of Sciences, National Academy of Engineering, and Institute of Medicine, 2007; *Rising Above The Gathering Storm: Energizing and Employing America for a Brighter Economic Future* (Washington, D.C., National Academies Press), 2007; www.nap.edu/openbook.php?record_id=11463&page=1; and Committee on Prospering in the Global Economy of the 21st Century: An Agenda for American Science and Technology, National Academy of Sciences, National Academy of Engineering, and Institute of Medicine *Rising Above the Gathering Storm, Revisited: Rapidly Approaching Category 5* (Washington, D.C.: National Academies Press, 2010), www.nap.edu/openbook.php?record_id=12999&page=1

[20] K. Arrow, Economic welfare and the allocation of resources for invention, in *The Rate and Direction of Inventive Activities,* edited by R. Nelson (Princeton: Princeton Univ. Press, 1962, 609–625).

[21] A. J. Salter and B. R. Martin, "The Economic Benefits of Publicly Funded Basic Research: A Critical Review," *Research Policy* 30 (2001):509–532.

[22] Z. Griliches, "R&D and Productivity," in *Handbook of Industrial Innovation*, ed. P. Stoneman (London: Blackwell, 1995, 52–89); Salter and Martin, op. cit.

[23] Salter and Martin, op. cit.

[24] Colin Macilwain, "What Science Is Really Worth," *Nature* 466 (2010): 682–684.

[25] Paul A. David, Bronwyn H. Hall, and Andrew A. Toole, "Is public R&D a complement or substitute for private R&D? A review of the econometric evidence," *Research Policy* 29 (2000), 497–529.

[26] Salter and Martin, op. cit.

[27] Ben R. Martin and Puay Tang, "The Benefits from Publicly Funded Research." In *SPRU Electronic Working Paper Series*, 2007; Andrew A. Toole, "The Impact of Public Basic Research on Industrial Innovation: Evidence from the Pharmaceutical Industry," Working Paper, 2008; Alston, "The Benefits from Agricultural Research and Development, Innovation, and Productivity Growth," *OECD Food, Agriculture and Fisheries Working Papers,* No. 31 (2010), OECD Publishing; Martin Buxton, Steve Hanney, and Teri Jones, "Estimating the Economic Value to Societies of the Impact of Health Research: A Critical Review," *Bulletin of the World Health Organization* 82 (10) (2004):733–739.

[28] For discussion of methodological issues, see Committee on Measuring Economic and Other Returns on Federal Research Investments, "Measuring the Impacts of Federal Investments in Research," National Academies Press, 2011.

[29] Further, Bush recognized that, before the war, the United States had depended on non-appropriable discoveries from abroad: "Basic scientific research is scientific capital. Moreover, we cannot any longer depend upon Europe as a major source of this scientific capital. Clearly, more and better scientific research is one essential to the achievement of our goal of full employment," (Bush, "Science," p. 6).

[30] "Gross Domestic Product 2010," World Development Indicators Database, World Bank, 1 July 2011 at sitere-sources.worldbank.org/DATASTATISTICS/Resources/GDP

[31] The World Wide Web is itself a spectacular example. Browser technology was invented by European physicists, but it was U.S. entrepreneurs who created the economic ecosystem that supports much of today's commerce.

[32] National Science Board, *Science and Engineering Indicators 2012*. Arlington VA: National Science Foundation (NSB 12-01), 2012. Appendix Table 2-21. Data are from 2009, the most recent available.

[33] Committee on Global Science and Technology Strategies and Their Effect on U.S. National Security, "S&T Strategies of Six Countries: Implications for the United States," National Academies Press, 2010.

[34] Bush, "Science."

[35] It is often repeated that Michael Faraday, when asked by Prime Minister William Gladstone about the usefulness of electromagnetism, replied, "Someday, sir, you can tax it." The story is almost surely apocryphal, but still enlightening. See http://www.snopes.com/quotes/faraday.asp

[36] In the technical literature, investments with this property are termed "long-tailed" or "fat-tailed." They can have the property that their largest returns come from their rarest events, in a way that makes their average rate of return mathematically infinite. Over any finite period of time the return is, of course, finite; but the longer you wait, the better it tends to get.

[37] Pew poll, op cit.

[38] National Science Board, "Science and Engineering Indicators 2012," Chapter 7, at http://www.nsf.gov/statistics

[39] "The Times Higher Education World University Rankings 2011–2012," TSL Education Ltd., 2012, at www.timeshighereducation.co.uk/world-university-rankings/2011-2012/top-400.html

[40] "Academic Ranking of World Universities," 2011 Shanghai Ranking Consultancy at www.shanghairanking.com/ARWU2011.html

[41] Fields Medals are widely considered as the Nobel Prizes of pure mathematics.

[42] Committee on Prospering in the Global Economy of the 21st Century: An Agenda for American Science and Technology, National Academy of Sciences, National Academy of Engineering, and Institute of Medicine, *Rising Above The Gathering Storm: Energizing and Employing America for a Brighter Economic Future* (Washington, D.C.: National Academies Press, 2007), www.nap.edu/openbook.php?record_id=11463&page=1

[43] Ibid.

[44] Alan S. Brown. "The Gathering Storm: Can the U.S. Preserve its Lead in Science & Technology?" www.tbp.org/pages/publications/Bent/Features/F06Brown.pdf

[45] OECD, "Where Do Students Go to Study Abroad?" in *Education at a Glance 2011: Highlights,* 2011, at www.oecd-ilibrary.org/docserver/download/fulltext/9611051ec013.pdf?expires=1325523346&id=id&accname=guest&checksum=C0E2EC02146BFEDD 86488DB643C474AB This study refers to all fields of study, not just the sciences, but is illustrative

[46] We use the term "Federal laboratories" as an umbrella term to describe Government-run, Government-operated laboratories and similar intramural research programs, including those at NIH. In some contexts, we also mean to include the (largely Federally supported) independent research institutes, such as the Broad Institute, Scripps Research Institute, Salk Institute, and Woods Hole Oceanographic Institute, to name a few. The term "National Laboratory," while having no legal definition, is intended to be inclusive of the DOE contractor-operated laboratories, and also the larger FFRDCs (generally with "National" in their name), such as NSF's NAIC, NCAR, NOAO, and NRAO. DoD's University Affiliated Research Centers (UARCs) could be considered as National Laboratories, but are operated each by a single university.

[47] Jet Propulsion Laboratory, "JPL History" at www.jpl.nasa.gov/jplhistory/

[48] FAR 35.017 at www.acquisition.gov/far/97-03/html/35.html

[49] National Science Board, *Science and Engineering Indicators 2012.*

[50] Battelle and R&D Magazine, "2012 Global R&D Funding Forecast," 2011, at battelle.org/docs/default-document-library/2012_global_forecast.pdf

[51] National Research Council, "Research Universities and the Future of America," 2012, at download.nap.edu/catalog.php?record_id=13299

[52] National Science Board, *Science and Engineering Indicators 2012.*

[53] National University of Singapore, Nanyang Technological University, and Singapore Management University.

[54] Singapore Government, Ministry of Education, International Academic Advisory Panel, Press Release, November 12, 2010, www.moe.gov.sg/media

[55] National Science Board, *Science and Engineering Indicators 2010* (Arlington VA: National Science Foundation, NSB 10-01).

[56] Adrian Slywotzky, "Where Have You Gone, Bell Labs?" *BusinessWeek*, August 27, 2009, at www.businessweek.com/magazine/content/09_36/b4145036681619.htm

[57] Ibid.

[58] Ibid.

[59] Robert Atkinson and Howard Wial, "Boosting Productivity, Innovation, and Growth through a National Innovation Foundation," April 2008.

[60] M. Hourihan and M. Stepp, "A Model for Innovation: ARPA-E Merits Full Funding," The Information Technology and Innovation Foundation, July 2011.

[61] National Science Board, *Science and Engineering Indicators 2010*, Appendix tables 4-8, 4-9, and 4-10.

[62] National Science Board, *Science and Engineering Indicators 2012*, www.nsf.gov/statistics

[63] JASON, "S&T for National Security," 2009, www.fas.org/irp/agency/dod/jason/sandt-full.pdf

[64] "PCAST Report to the President on Ensuring American Leadership in Advanced Manufacturing," June 2011 at http://www.whitehouse.gov/sites/default/files/microsites/ostp/pcast-advanced-manufacturing-june2011.pdf

[65] Joe Light, "More Companies Plan to Put R&D Overseas," *The Wall Street Journal*, February 22, 2011, online.wsj.com/article/SB10001424052748703803904576152543358840066.html

[66] CEO of major U.S. chemical company, personal communication.

[67] "R&D by Multinational Companies," *Science and Engineering Indicators 2012* at www.nsf.gov/statistics

[68] F. Block and M. Keller, "Where do Innovations Come From? Transformations in the U.S. National Innovation System, 1970–2006," The Information Technology and Innovation Foundation, 2008.

[69] National Science Board, *Science and Engineering Indicators 2010*, Figure 5-28 at www.nsf.gov/statistics

[70] "PCAST Report to the President on Ensuring American Leadership in Advanced Manufacturing," June 2011 at www.whitehouse.gov/sites/default/files/microsites/ostp/pcast-advanced-manufacturing

[71] Battelle and R&D Magazine, "2012 Global R&D Funding Forecast," 2011, at battelle.org/docs/default-document-library/2012_global_forecast.pdf

[72] Land Grant College Act, 7 U.S.C. § 301 et seq.

[73] Agricultural College Act of 1890, 26 Stat. 417, 7 U.S.C. § 321 et seq.

[74] Richard C. Atkinson and William A. Blanpied, "Research Universities: Core of the US Science and Technology System," *Technology in Society* 30 (2008): 30–48, at http://www.rca.ucsd.edu/speeches/TIS_ResearchUniversitiesCoreoftheUSscienceandtechnologysystem1.pdf

[75] Ibid.

[76] Bush, "Science."

[77] Ibid.

[78] Then called the National Institute of Health, NIH had been created in 1930 by the Ransdell Act from the older Laboratory of Hygiene. See history

[79] Leslie Tolbert, VP for research at the University of Arizona, as quoted in David Kramer, "Will Industry Save Academic Research?" *Physics Today,* September 2011, p. 28, at www.physicstoday.org/resource/1/phtoad/v64/i9/p28_s1

[80] "Dow Commits $25 Million per Year to Advance Research & Development in Leading U.S. Universities," October 2011, at www.dow.com/innovation/pdf/partnership/20111004a.pdf

[81] Gary Chapman, "Rep. Brown Left a Legacy for Science," *Los Angeles Times,* August 02, 1999.

[82] Kauffman Foundation, "Proof of Concept Centers: Accelerating the Commercialization of University Innovation," 2008, at sites.kauffman.org/pdf/poc_centers_01242008.pdf

[83] "U of Utah Ranks First with MIT at Starting Companies," February 16, 2010, at unews.utah.edu/old/p/021610-2.html

[84] National Science Foundation, Division of Science Resources Statistics, "National Patterns of R&D Resources: 2008 Data Update," NSF 10-314, Arlington, VA, 2010, www.nsf.gov/statistics

[85] MIT Industry Guide, Industrial Liaison Program, webMassachusetts Institute of Technology, " Reports to the President," 2010, 24–27, web.mit.edu/ annualreports/pres10/2010.24.00.pdf

[86] Association of University Technology Managers (AUTM), "AUTM U.S. Licensing Activity Survey: FY2010 Summary: A Survey Summary of Technology Licensing Activity for U.S. Academic and Nonprofit Institutions and Technology Investment Firms," edited by Rich Kordal, Paul Hippenmeyer, and Arjun Sanga, 2011. See also Robert D. Atkinson and Scott M. Andes, *The 2008 State New Economy Index: Benchmarking Economic Transformation in the States* (Washington, DC: Information Technology and Innovation Foundation, 2008, 64), www.itif.org/publications/2008-state

[87] The Science Coalition, "Sparking Economic Growth: How Federally Funded University Research Creates Innovation, New Companies and Jobs," Washington D.C., 2010, www.sciencecoalition.org/successstories/fullReport.cfm

[88] "Energy Biosciences Institute: Highlights of the Master Agreement." UC Berkeley News, November 14, 2007, berkeley.edu/news/media

[89] National Council of University Research Administrators, "Sponsored Projects and Technology Transfer: Working Together to Build Successful and Effective Industry-University Cooperative Research Centers," November 2010, www.ncura.edu/content/educational_programs/sites/52/docs/T_1030_G1.pptx

[90] Subra Suresh, "Talking Points on the National Science Foundation's Innovation Corps to Strengthen the Impact of Scientific Discoveries," National Science Foundation, July 28, 2011, at www.nsf.gov/news/speeches/suresh/11/ss110728_icorps.jsp

[91] Available at www.itrs.net/

[92] "Amgen Ventures," www.amgen.com/partners/amgen_ventures.html

[93] "IBM, SignalDemand Team With ConAgra Mills to Help Customers Adapt to Shifting Market Conditions With Analytics," www-03.ibm.com/press/us/en/pressrelease/35955.wss

[94] Federal Laboratory Consortium for Technology Transfer, "About the FLC," 2012, www. federallabs.org/home/about/

[95] Office of Laboratory Policy and Evaluation and National Nuclear Security Administration, "Annual Report on Technology Transfer and Related Technology Partnering Activities at the National Laboratories and Other Facilities Fiscal Years 2007 and 2008, 2009," U.S. Department of Energy, Washington, D.C., techtrans- fer.energy

[96] Presidential Memorandum, "Accelerating Technology Transfer and Commercialization of Federal Research in Support of High-Growth Businesses," October 28, 2011, www. whitehouse.gov/the-press-office/2011/10/28/presidential-memorandum-accelerating-technology

[97] LANL, "Los Alamos–Proctor and Gamble Partnership Advances," www.lanl.gov/orgs/tt/pdf/ partnering/pg.pdf; Pete Engardio, "Los Alamos and Sandia: R&D Treasures," *Bloomberg BusinessWeek,* September 11, 2008, www.businessweek.com/magazine/content/08_38/ b4100062751339.htm

[98] "Department of Energy Awards $156 Million for Groundbreaking Energy Research Projects." *ARPA-E News,* September 29, 2011, at arpa-e.energy

[99] The Biomarker Consortium. Consortium Partners, at www.biomarkersconsortium.org/ consortium.php

[100] Mark Weisbrot, "2016: when China overtakes the US," *The Guardian*, April 27, 2011, www. guardian

[101] Mark Boroush, "U.S. R&D Spending Suffered a Rare Decline in 2009 but Outpaced the Overall Economy," NSF NCSES, March 2012, at www.nsf.gov/statistics

[102] We are pleased that the President's 2013 budget submission reasserted the goal in principle, even if the time scale is uncertain.

[103] ACQuipedia, Department of Defense, "Future Years Defense Program (FYDP)" at acc.dau. mil/CommunityBrowser.aspx?id=362504

[104] General Accounting Office, "Multiyear Authorizations for Research and Development," June 3, 1981, at www.gao.gov/assets/140/133388.pdf

[105] National Science Board, *Science and Engineering Indicators 2012.*

[106] *Organization for Economic Cooperation and Development (OECD) Science, Technology and Industry Scoreboard of 2007;* Robert D. Atkinson and Scott M. Andes, "U.S. Continues to Tread Water in Global R&D Tax Incentives," Information Technology & Innovation Foundation, August 12, 2009; Deloitte's "Global Survey of R&D Tax Incentives 2011."

[107] The Information Technology and Innovation Foundation (ITIF), "United States Lags Far Behind in R&D Tax Incentive Generosity," July 2012, at http://www2.itif.org/2012-were-27-b-index-tax.pdf

[108] PCAST, "Report to the President on Ensuring American Leadership in Advanced Manufacturing," June 2011.

[109] Robert D. Atkinson, "Create Jobs by Expanding the R&D Tax Credit," technical report, ITIF, 2010, www.itif.org/files/2010-01-26-RandD.pdf

[110] Executive Office of the President. 2012. *Budget of the United States Government, Fiscal Year 2013.*

[111] See, for example, "Sen. Coons Calls for Making R&D Tax Credit Permanent, Open to Start-ups," The Hill, at thehill.com/blogs

[112] Federal Demonstration Partnership. "A Profile of Federal-Grant Administrative Burden Among Federal Demonstration Partnership Faculty," 2007.

[113] National Institutes of Health, "Research Project Success Rates by NIH Institute for 2011," Research Portfolio Online Reporting Tools (RePORT), 2012, report.nih.gov/success_rates/Success_ByIC.cfm

[114] NIH Notices NOT-OD-07-017 and NOT-OD-11-118. See grants.nih.gov/grants/guide/notice-files/NOT-OD-11-118.html

[115] Tobin L. Smith, Josh Trapani, Anthony DeCrappeo, and David Kennedy, "Reforming Regulation of Research Universities," *Issues in Science and Technology,* Summer Edition, 2011.

[116] "Exec. Order No. 13563–Improving Regulation and Regulatory Review," *Fed. Reg.,* Vol 76, No 14 (Jan. 18, 2011), at www.whitehouse.gov/the-press-office/2011/01/18/improving-regulation-and-regulatory-review-executive-order

[117] Association of American Universities, Association of Public and Land-grant Universities, and the Council on Governmental Relations, "Regulatory and Financial Reform of Federal Research Policy Recommendations to the NRC Committee on Research Universities," 2011; Council on Governmental Relations, "Federal Funding Agency Limitations on Cost Reimbursement: A Request for Consistency in the Application of Federal Guidelines," 2010; Tobin L. Smith, Josh Trapani, Anthony DeCrappeo, and David Kennedy, "Reforming Regulation of Research Universities," *Issues in Science and Technology,* Summer Edition, 2011; and Committee on Research Universities, National Research Council, "Breaking Through: Ten Strategic Actions to Leverage Our Research Universities for the Future of America," 2012.

[118] Association of American Universities, Association of Public and Land-grant Universities, and the Council on Governmental Relations, "Regulatory and Financial Reform of Federal Research Policy Recommendations to the NRC Committee on Research Universities," 2011; Tobin L. Smith, Josh Trapani, Anthony DeCrappeo, and David Kennedy, "Reforming Regulation of Research Universities," *Issues in Science and Technology,* Summer Edition, 2011.

[119] For example, the Baldridge Performance Excellence Program administered by NIST, or the international ISO 9000 process.

[120] OMB, "CIRCULAR A-110 REVISED 11/19/93 As Further Amended 9/30/99," at www.whitehouse.gov/omb/circulars_a110#23

[121] National Science Board, "Science and Engineering Indicators 2012,". Arlington VA: National Science Foundation (NSB 12-01), 2012, Figure 2-B. State appropriations for public research universities per enrolled student: 2002-10, www.nsf.gov/statistics

[122] University of California, "The Facts: UC Budget Basics," UC Office of the President, November 2011, at budget.universityofcalifornia.edu/files/2011/12/Budget_fact_11.29.11.pdf

[123] National Science Board, "Research and Development, Innovation, and the Science and Engineering Workforce," July 2012, at nsf.gov/nsb/publications/2012/nsb1203.pdf

[124] Nicholas Johnson, Phil Oliff, and Erica Williams, "An Update on State Budget Cuts," Center on Budget and Policy Priorities, February 9, 2011, at www.cbpp.org/cms/index.cfm?fa=view&id=1214

[125] National Science Foundation, National Center for Science and Engineering Statistics, "Research and Development Expenditures: Fiscal Year 2009," NSF 11-313, Arlington, VA, 2011, Table 1. R&D Expenditures at universities and colleges, by source of funds: FY 1953–2009, www.nsf.gov/statistics

[126] U.S. Department of Education, National Center for Education Statistics, "The Condition of Education 2011," NCES 2011-033, 2011, Table A-50-1, A-50-3, nces.ed.gov/pubs2011/2011033.pdf. This number is found by dividing the total 2008–2009 expenditures on research by all postsecondary institutions by the total 2008–2009 revenues from tuition and fees by all postsecondary institutions.

[127] National Science Board, "Investing in the Future: NSF Cost Sharing Policies for a Robust Federal Research Enterprise," NSB-09-20 (Arlington VA: National Science Foundation, 2009), at www.nsf.gov/pubs/2009/nsb0920/nsb0920.pdf

[128] National Science Foundation, "Implementation of the 2nd NSB Cost Sharing Report: NSF Revised Cost Sharing Policy Statement," at www.nsf.gov/bfa/dias/policy

[129] "Cost Sharing DOE Financial Assistance Awards," at www.eere-pmc.energy

[130] "Report to the President on Accelerating the Pace of Change in Energy Technologies Through an Integrated Federal Energy Policy," at www.whitehouse.gov/sites/default/files/microsites/ostp/pcast-energy

[131] The word "incremental" has unfairly acquired a derogatory connotation that we do not agree with. Evolutionary (or incremental) research is the bedrock of scientific advance.

[132] Arden L Bement Jr. "Transformative Research: The Artistry and Alchemy of the 21st Century," delivered on Jan. 4, 2007, at www.nsf.gov/news/speeches/bement/07/alb070104_texas.jsp; NIH, "NIH Director Announces Enhancements to Peer Review," at www.nih.gov/news/healthAmerican Academy of Arts and Sciences, *ARISE 1: Advancing Research In Science and Engineering: Investing in Early-Career Scientists and High-Risk, High-Reward Research* (Cambridge, Massachusetts, 2008); NSB, "Enhancing Support of Transformative Research at the National Science Foundation," at www.nsf.gov/nsb/documents/2007/tr_report.pdf; NRC, "Research Universities and the Future of America," 2012, at www.nap.edu/catalog.php?record_id=13396#toc; and National Science Foundation, "Hearing Summary–Investing in High-Risk, High-Reward Research," NSF and Congress, October 8, 2009, at www.nsf.gov/about/congress; National Institutes of Health, "Enhancing Peer Review at NIH," March 25, 2011, at enhancing-peer-review.nih.gov/

[133] American Academy of Arts and Sciences, *ARISE 1,* p. 36.

[134] NSB, at www.nsf.gov/nsb/documents/2007/tr_report.pdf, p. 9.

[135] NSF, "Empowering the Nation through Discovery and Innovation–NSF Strategic Plan for Fiscal Years 2011–2016," at www.nsf.gov/news/strategicplan/nsfstrategicplan_2011_2016.pdf

[136] NSF, "CREATIV: Creative Research Awards for Transformative Interdisciplinary Ventures" at www.nsf.gov/pubs/2012/nsf12011/nsf12011.jsp

[137] American Academy of Arts and Sciences, *ARISE 1*, p. 32.

[138] "NIH Director's Early Independence Awards (DP5) Request for Proposals," Health and Human Services, 2011, at grantsand "2012 NIH Director's New Innovator Award Program (DP2), Request for Proposals," 2011, Health and Human Services grants.nih.gov/grants/guide/rfa-files/RFA-RM-11-005.html

[139] "Congressional Justification of the NIH fiscal year (FY) 2012 Budget Request," National Institutes of Health, at officeofbudget.od.nih.gov/pdfs/FY12/Volume%201%20-%20Overview.pdf

[140] Data provided to PCAST from IDA Science and Technology Policy Institute.

[141] National Science Foundation, "Phase II: Proposal Review and Processing," at www.nsf.gov/bfa/dias/policy

[142] NIH, "Rock Talk: Paylines, Percentiles and Success Rates," at nexus.od.nih.gov/all/2011/02/15/paylines-percentiles-success-rates/

[143] James Turner, "Best Practices in Merit Review: A Report to the U.S. Department of Energy," Association of Public and Land Grant Universities, 2010, at www.aplu.org/document.doc?id=2948

[144] Presidential Early Career Award recipients, who are chosen from CAREER recipient, as well as early career awardees at NIH and other agencies, are the elite of the elite.

[145] The external panel, co-chaired by Drs. Keith Yamamoto and Lawrence Tabak, is often referred to as the Yama-moto Committee; NIH, "Enhancing Peer Review Initiative," 2007, at enhancing-peer-review.nih.gov/; and NIH, "Peer Review Process and Changes," 2009, at enhancing-peer-review.nih.gov/process&changes.html

[146] For example, Ferric C. Fang and Arturo Casadevall, "NIH Peer Review Reform—Change We Need, or Lipstick on a Pig?" *Infect. Immun.*, vol. 77 (2009), no. 3, pp. 929–32.

[147] NIH, "Revised New and Early Stage Investigator Policies," NOT-OD-09-013, 2008, at grants.nih.gov/grants/guide/notice-files/not-od-09-013.html

[148] PCAST, *Prepare and Inspire: K-12 Education in Science, Technology, Engineering, and Math (STEM) for America's Future,* September 2010, at www.whitehouse.gov/sites/default/files/microsites/ostp/pcast-stemed-report.pdf; PCAST, *Engage to Excel,* at www.whitehouse.gov/sites/default/files/microsites/ostp/pcast-engage-to-excel-final_feb.pdf

[149] PCAST, *Prepare and Inspire.*

[150] AAU Undergraduate Stem Education Initiative at www.aau.edu/policy

[151] Higher Education Research Institute at UCLA, "Degrees of Success: Bachelor's Degree Completion Rates among Initial STEM Majors," 2010, at www.heri.ucla.edu/nih/downloads/2010%20-%20Hurtado,%20Eagan,%20Chang%20-%20Degrees%20of%20Success.pdf

[152] Cornell Higher Education Research Institute, "2011 Survey of Differential Tuition at Public Higher Education Institutions," at www.ilr.cornell.edu/cheri/upload/2011CHERISurveyFinal0212.pdf

[153] "Building a 21st Century Immigration System," at www.whitehouse.gov/sites/default/files/rss_viewer/immigration

[154] Ibid.

[155] "American Made: The Impact of Immigrant Entrepreneurs and Professionals on U.S. Competitiveness," at www.nvca.org/index.php?option=com_content&view=article&id=254&Itemid=103

[156] Video transcript of January 2011 PCAST public meeting, at www.tvworldwide.com/events/pcast/110107/default.cfm (at 21:20).

[157] U.S. Department of Homeland Security/U.S. Immigration and Customs Enforcement, "ICE Announces Expanded List of Science, Technology, Engineering, and Math Degree Programs: Qualifies Eligible Graduates to Extend Their Post-Graduate Training," 2011, at www.ice.gov/news/releases/1105/110512washingtondc2.htm; U.S Department of Homeland Security/U.S. Immigration and Customs Enforcement, "DHS Announces Expanded List of STEM Degree Programs," 2012.

[158] PCAST, "Report to the President and Congress on the Third Assessment of the National Nanotechnology Initiative," 2010, 30, www.whitehouse.gov/sites/default/files/microsites/ostp/pcast-nni-report.pdf

[159] PCAST, 2011. "Report to the President on Ensuring American Leadership in Advanced Manufacturing," www.whitehouse.gov/sites/default/files/microsites/ostp/pcast-advanced-manufacturing

[160] 15 C.F.R. § 734.8, at ecfr.gpoaccess.gov/cgi/t/text/text-idx?c=ecfr&sid=e12e954f764c8858b67d1be3219d1eae&rgn=div5&view=text&node=15:2.1.3.4.22&idno=15#15:2.1.3.4.22.0.1.8

[161] Memo from AAAS, AAU, APLU, and COGR to Departments of Commerce and State, at cstsp.aaas.org/files/CommentLetter020711.pdf

[162] "Wes Bush Address to Association for Unmanned Vehicle Systems International," at www.northropgrumman.com/presentations/2011/081711-wes-bush-at-auvsi-2011-forum.html

[163] "GM, Argonne Sign Licensing Deal for Advanced Battery Chemistry," at www.anl.gov/Media_Center/News/2011/news110106.html

[164] Battelle Ventures, at www.battelleventures.com/

[165] "FDA-Approved Products Based on NIH Intramural Research," at www.ott.nih.gov/ about_nih/fda_approved_products.aspx

[166] M. E. Hughes, S. V. Howieson, G. Walejko, N. Gupta, S. Jonas, A. T. Brenner, D. Holmes, E. Shyu, and S. Shipp, "Technology Transfer and Commercialization Landscape of the Federal Laboratories," IDA Paper NS P-4728 (Alexandria, VA: Institute for Defense Analyses, June 2001), www.ida.org/upload/stpi/pdfs/p-4728nsfinal508compliantfedlabttcreport.pdf

[167] National Science Board, *Science and Engineering Indicators 2012.*

[168] Council on Graduate Schools, "Pathways Through Graduate School and Into Careers," at www.pathwaysreport.org/

[169] NSF, "Integrative Graduate Education and Research Traineeship Program (IGERT)," at www.nsf.gov/funding

[170] The Kauffman Foundation identified programs at more than 50 universities in the United States, awarding more than $10 million in prizes. See www.kauffman.org/newsroom/new-hub

[171] Maureen Farrell. "The Biggest Small Business Competitions," Forbes, 2010, at www.forbes.com/2010/01/26/small-business-competition

[172] Master of Entrepreneurship Program, at entrepreneurship.umich.edu

[173] PCAST, *Engage to Excel.*

[174] University of Texas at Austin, Freshman Research Initiatives, at fri.cns.utexas.edu

[175] University of Michigan Undergraduate Research Opportunity Program at www.lsa.umich.edu/urop/

[176] NSF Research Experience for Undergraduates Program, at www.nsf.gov/pubs/2009/nsf09598/nsf09598.htm

[177] *Technology Transfer, Administration of the Bayh-Dole Act by Research Universities*, U.S. Government Accounting Office Report to Congressional Committees, May, 1998.

[178] "Innovation's Golden Goose," *Economist Technology Quarterly,* Dec. 12, 2002, at www.economist.com/node/1476653

[179] "Managing University Intellectual Property in the Public Interest," National Research Council, 2010.

[180] "The University of Michigan Technology Transfer Policy," at www.techtransfer.umich.edu/resources

[181] University of Minnesota, "Industry-Sponsored Research: Minnesota Innovation Partnerships (MN-IP)," at www.research.umn.edu/techcomm/industry

[182] Joe Petrucci, "Keystone Edge," December 15, 2011, at www.keystoneedge.com/features/pennstateintellectualproperty1215.aspx

[183] AUTM, "AUTM U.S. Licensing Activity Survey: FY2010 Summary."

[184] GoogleCrumbs, December 2, 2005, at www.googlecrumbs.com/2005/12/02/stanford-earns-336-million-from-google

[185] See Section 521 of the bill, at www.gpo.gov/fdsys/pkg/BILLS-111hr5116enr/pdf/BILLS-111hr5116enr.pdf

[186] National Institutes of Health National Center for Advancing Translational Sciences, at www.ncats.nih.gov/

[187] We can add further examples: the University of Dundee's "Dundee Kinase Consortium" in the U.K., and in the United States, on a smaller scale, the Alzheimer's Disease Neuroimaging Initiative, the Biomarker Consortium, the Cardiac Safety Research Consortium, the Patient Reported Outcomes Consortium, the Analgesic Clinical Trials Innovation Opportunities and Network (ACTION), the Predictive Safety Consortium, and the Se- rious Adverse Events Consortium.

[188] NIH NCATS, "Clinical and Translational Science Awards," at www.ncats.nih.gov/research/cts/ctsa/ctsa.html

[189] See Paula Stephan, "Perverse incentives," *Nature,* vol. 484, p. 29 (April 5, 2012), for a thoughtful discussion of the issue.

[190] See Doug Lederman "Baby Steps on Speeding up the Ph.D.," *Inside Higher Ed,* March, 28, 2006, and references therein, at www.insidehighered.com/news/2006/03/28/phd

[191] "Science Resources Statistics Infobrief: Time to Degree of U.S. Research Doctorate Recipients," at www.nsf.gov/statistics

[192] See Figure 3 in "NIH, Advisory Committee to the NIH Director, Biomedical Workforce Task Force," at acd.od.nih.gov/bwf.htm

[193] "Research Training in the Biomedical, Behavioral, and Clinical Research Sciences," at www.nap.edu/catalog.php?record_id=12983

[194] NSF, "Employment Sector of S&E Highest Degree Holders and S&E Doctorate Holders: 2008," *S&E Indicators 2012,* http://www.nsf.gov/statistics

[195] "NIH, Advisory Committee to the NIH Director, Biomedical Workforce Task Force," acd.od.nih.gov/bwf.htm

[196] "Addressing the Nation's Changing Needs for Biomedical and Behavioral Scientists," at grants1.nih.gov/training

[197] Association of American Medical Colleges, "NIH Issues FY 2012 Fiscal Policy; NRSA Stipends Increase by Two Percent," www.aamc.org/advocacy

[198] NSF, "2009 Survey of Earned Doctorates," www.nsf.gov/statistics

[199] PCAST, "Report to the President on Accelerating the Pace of Change in Energy Technologies Through an Integrated Federal Energy Policy," at www.whitehouse.gov/sites/default/files/microsites/ostp/pcast-energyPCAST, "Report to the President and Congress on the Third Assessment of the National Nanotechnology Initiative," at www.whitehouse.gov/sites/default/files/microsites/ostp/pcast-nni-report.pdf; PCAST, "Report to the President and Congress on the Fourth Assessment of the National Nanotechnology Initiative," at www.whitehouse.gov/sites/default/files/microsites/ostp/PCAST_2012_Nanotechnology_FINAL.pdf; PCAST, "Report to the President and Congress: Designing A Digital Future: Federally Funded Research and Development in Networking and Information Technology," at www.nitrd.gov/pcast-2010/report/nitrd-program/pcast-nitrd-report-2010.pdf PCAST, "Report to the President on Ensuring American Leadership in Advanced Manufacturing," June 2011, at www.whitehouse.gov/sites/default/files/microsites/ostp/pcast-advanced-manufacturing PCAST Report to the President Sustaining Environmental Capital: Protecting Society and the Economy," at www.whitehouse.gov/sites/default/files/microsites/ostp/pcast_sustaining_environmental_capital_report.pdf PCAST, *Prepare and Inspire*; and PCAST, *Engage to Excel.*

[200] American Academy of Arts and Sciences, *ARISE 1*

[201] National Research Council, "Research Universities and the Future of America," 2012, at hdownload.nap.edu/catalog.php?record_id=13299

[202] "NIH, Advisory Committee to the NIH Director, Biomedical Workforce Task Force," acd.od.nih.gov/bwf.htm

[203] National Science Board, "Research and Development, Innovation, and the Science and Engineering Workforce," July 2012, nsf.gov/nsb/publications/2012/nsb1203.pdf

[204] AAU, APLU, COGR, "Regulatory and Financial Reform of Federal Research Policy: Recommendations to the NRC Committee on Research Universities," at energy.gov/sites/prod/files/gcprod/documents/RFIRegReview_CouncilGovtRelationsAppendix_03212011.pdf

[205] Business Roundtable, "Taking Action for America: A CEO Plan for Jobs and Economic Growth," at business-roundtable.org/studies-and-reports/taking-action-for-america

In: The United States Research Enterprise
Editor: Daniel S. Rosser
ISBN: 978-1-62417-916-7

Chapter 2

INDUSTRIAL COMPETITIVENESS AND TECHNOLOGICAL ADVANCEMENT: DEBATE OVER GOVERNMENT POLICY*

Wendy H. Schacht

SUMMARY

There is ongoing interest in the pace of U.S. technological advancement due to its influence on U.S. economic growth, productivity, and international competitiveness. Because technology can contribute to economic growth and productivity increases, congressional attention has focused on how to augment private-sector technological development. Legislative activity over the past 30 or more years has created a policy for technology development, albeit an ad hoc one. Because of the lack of consensus on the scope and direction of a national policy, Congress has taken an incremental approach aimed at creating new mechanisms to facilitate technological advancement in particular areas and making changes and improvements as necessary.

Congressional action has mandated specific technology development programs and obligations in federal agencies. Many programs were created based upon what individual committees judged appropriate within the agencies over which they had authorization or appropriation responsibilities. However,

* This is an edited, reformatted and augmented version of the Congressional Research Service Publication, CRS Report for Congress RL33528, dated December 3, 2012.

there has been recent legislative activity directed at eliminating or significantly curtailing many of these federal efforts. Several programs have been terminated and the budgets for other initiatives have declined.

The proper role of the federal government in technology development and the competitiveness of U.S. industry continues to be a topic of congressional debate. Legislation affecting the research and development (R&D) environment has included both direct and indirect measures to facilitate technological innovation. In general, direct measures are those which involve budget outlays and the provision of services by government agencies. Indirect measures include financial incentives and legal changes (e.g., liability or regulatory reform; new antitrust arrangements). As the Congress develops its appropriation priorities, the manner by which the government encourages technological progress in the private sector again may be explored and/or redefined.

TECHNOLOGY AND COMPETITIVENESS

Technological advancement in U.S. industry often has been supported by congressional initiatives over the past 30 or more years. This approach has involved both direct measures that concern budget outlays and the provision of services by government agencies (such as the now terminated Advanced Technology Program (ATP) and the Technology Innovation Program (TIP), as well as the existing Manufacturing Extension Partnership (MEP) of the National Institute of Standards and Technology) and indirect measures that include financial incentives and legal changes. Many of these efforts, however, have been revisited over the past several congresses. Congressional legislation appears to have favored indirect strategies such as tax policies, intellectual property right protection, and antitrust laws to promote technological advancement and government support for basic research over direct federal funding for private sector technology commercialization initiatives.

Interest in technology development and industrial innovation increased as concern mounted over the economic strength of the nation and over competition from abroad. For the United States to be competitive in the world economy, U.S. companies must be able to engage in trade, retain market shares, and offer high quality products, processes, and services while the nation maintains economic growth and a high standard of living. Technological advancement is important because the commercialization of inventions provides economic benefits from the sale of new products or services; from new ways to provide a service; or from new processes that increase productivity and efficiency. It is widely accepted that technological progress is responsible for up to one-half the growth of the U.S. economy, and is one principal driving force in long-term growth and increases in living standards.

Technological advances can further economic growth because they contribute to the creation of new goods, new services, new jobs, and new capital. The application of technology can improve productivity and the quality of products. It can expand the range of services that can be offered as well as extend the geographic distribution of these services. The development and use of technology also plays a major role in determining patterns of international trade by affecting the comparative advantages of industrial sectors. Since technological progress is not necessarily determined by economic conditions—it also can be influenced by advances in science, the organization and management of firms, government activity, or serendipity—it can have effects on trade independent of shifts in macroeconomic factors. New technologies also can help compensate for possible disadvantages in the cost of capital and labor faced by firms.

THE FEDERAL ROLE IN TECHNOLOGY DEVELOPMENT

American companies have faced increased competitive pressures in the international marketplace from firms based in countries where governments actively promote commercial technological development and application. In the United States, the generation of technology for the commercial marketplace is primarily a private sector activity. The federal government traditionally becomes involved only for certain limited purposes. Typically these are activities which have been determined to be necessary for the "national good" but which cannot, or will not, be supported by industry.

To date, the U.S. government has funded research and development (R&D) to meet the mission requirements of the federal departments and agencies. It also finances efforts in areas where there is an identified need for research, primarily basic research, not being performed in the private sector. Federal support reflects a consensus that basic research is critical because it is the foundation for many new innovations. However, any returns created by this activity are generally long term, sometimes not marketable, and not always evident. Yet the rate of return to society as a whole generated by investments in research is significantly larger than the benefits that can be captured by the firm doing the work.[1]

Many past government activities to increase basic research were based on a "linear" model of innovation. This theory viewed technological advancement as a series of sequential steps starting with idea origination and moving through basic research, applied research, development, commercialization, and diffusion into the economy. Increases in federal funds in the basic research stage were expected to result in concomitant increases in new products and processes. However, this linear concept is no longer considered valid. Innovations often occur that do not require basic or applied research or development; in fact many innovations are incremental improvements to existing products or processes. In certain areas, such as biotechnology, the distinctions between basic research and commercialization are small and shrinking. In others, the differentiation between basic and applied research is artificial. The critical factor is the *commercialization* of the technology. Economic benefits accrue only when a technology or technique is brought to the marketplace where it can be sold to generate income or applied to increase productivity. Yet, while the United States has a strong basic research enterprise, foreign firms appear equally, if not more, adept at taking the results of these scientific efforts and making commercially viable products. Often U.S. companies are competing in the global marketplace against goods and services developed by foreign industries from research performed in the United States. Thus, there has been increased congressional interest in mechanisms to accelerate the development and commercialization processes in the private sector.

The development of a governmental effort to facilitate technological advance has been particularly difficult because of the absence of a consensus on the need for an articulated policy. Technology demonstration and commercialization have traditionally been considered private sector functions in the United States. While over the years there have been various programs and policies to facilitate such activities (such as tax credits, technology transfer to industry, and patents), the approach had been ad hoc and uncoordinated. Many of the programs implemented were based upon what individual committees judged appropriate for the agencies over which they have jurisdiction. Despite the importance of technology to the economy, technology-related considerations often have not been integrated into economic decisions.

There have been attempts to provide a central focus for governmental activity in technology matters. P.L. 100-519 created within the Department of

Commerce a Technology Administration headed by a new Under Secretary for Technology. However, this office was abolished as of the end of FY2007 by the America Competes Act. To date, technological issues and responsibilities remain shared among many departments and agencies. This diffused focus has sometimes resulted in actions which, if not at cross purposes, may not have accounted for the impact of policies or practices in one area on other parts of the process. Technology issues involve components which operate both separately and in concert. While a diffused approach can offer varied responses to varied issues, the importance of interrelationships may be underestimated and their usefulness may suffer.

Several times, Congress has examined the idea of an industrial policy to develop a coordinated approach on issues of economic growth and industrial competitiveness. Technological advance is both one aspect of this and an altogether separate consideration. In looking at the development of an identified policy for industrial competitiveness, advocates argue that such an effort could ameliorate much of the uncertainty with which the private sector perceives future government actions. Some commentators maintain that consideration and delineation of national objectives could encourage industry to engage in more long-term planning with regard to R&D and to make decisions as to the best allocation of resources. Such a technology policy could generate greater consistency in government activities. Because technological development involves numerous risks, efforts to minimize uncertainty regarding federal programs and policies may help alleviate some of the disincentives perceived by industry.

The development of a technology policy, however, is a contentious issue. There is widespread resistance to what could be and has been called national planning, due variously to doubts as to its efficacy, to fear of adverse effects on our market system, to political beliefs about government intervention in our economic system, and to the current emphasis on short-term returns in both the political and economic arenas. Opponents of a national industrial policy may see this approach as government interference in the marketplace to "pick winners and losers." Instead, it is argued, measures that would occasion a better investment environment for industry to expand innovation-related efforts would be preferable to government decisionmaking in technological advancement.

Consideration of what constitutes government policy (both in terms of the industrial policy and technology policy) covers a broad range of ideas from laissez-faire to special government incentives to target specific high-technology, high-growth industries. Suggestions have been made for the creation of federal mechanisms to identify and support strategic industries and technologies. Various federal agencies and private sector groups have developed critical technology lists. However, others maintain that such targeting is an unwanted, and unwarranted, interference in the private sector which will cause unnecessary dislocations in the marketplace or a misallocation of resources. From their perspective, the government does not have the knowledge or expertise to make business-related decisions. Instead, they argue, the appropriate role for government is to encourage innovative activities in all industries and to keep market related decisionmaking within the business community that has ultimate responsibility for commercialization and where such decisions have traditionally been made.

The relationship between government and industry often is a major factor affecting innovation and the environment within which technological development takes place. This relationship can be adversarial, with the government acting to regulate or restrain the business community, rather than to facilitate its positive contributions to the nation. However, this may be changing as the benefits of industry/government cooperation become more apparent. There are an increasing number of areas where the traditional distinctions between public and private sector functions and responsibilities are becoming blurred. Many assumptions have been questioned, particularly in light of the increased internationalization of the U.S. economy. The business sector is no longer viewed in an exclusively domestic context; the economy of the United States is often tied to the economies of other nations. The technological superiority long held by the United States in many areas has been challenged by other industrialized countries in which economic, social, and political policies and practices foster government-industry cooperation in technological development.

The approach taken by the former Clinton Administration was a divergence from the past. Articulated in two reports issued in February 1993 (*A Vision of Change for America and Technology for America's Economic Growth, A New Direction to Build Economic Strength*),[2] the proposal called for a national commitment to, and a strategy for, technological advancement as part of a defined national economic policy. This detailed strategy offered a policy agenda for economic growth in the United States, of which technological development and industrial competitiveness were critical components.

The approach initially recommended and subsequently followed by the Clinton Administration provided a wide range of options while for the most part reflecting then current trends in congressional efforts to facilitate industrial advancement. This policy, backed by congressional legislation, increased federal coordination and augmented direct government spending for technological development. While many past activities focused primarily on research, the new initiatives shifted the emphasis toward *development* of new products, processes, and services by the private sector for the commercial marketplace. In addition, a significant number of the proposals aimed to increase both government and private sector support for R&D leading to the commercialization of technology.

Recent congresses and the Bush Administration questioned this approach. Instead, policies appeared more supportive of indirect strategies such as tax incentives, intellectual property protection, and antitrust laws to promote technology advancement, increased government support for basic research, and decreased direct federal funding for private sector technology activities. In the 2006 State of the Union Address, former President Bush announced the "American Competitiveness Initiative" to facilitate innovation and provide "our nation's children a firm grounding in math and science." To achieve these goals, the President called for doubling over the next 10 years the amount of federal funding for basic research, particularly in the National Science Foundation, the Office of Science in the Department of Energy, and in the core programs of the National Institute of Standards and Technology, Department of Commerce. In addition, the Initiative would increase the number of math and science teachers and make permanent the research and experiment tax credit.

In April 2009, President Obama indicated his decision to double the budget of the key science agencies, as identified by former President Bush, over the next 10 years. In President Obama's FY2011 budget the timeframe for doubling slipped to 11 years; his FY2012 budget was intentionally silent on a timeframe for doubling. In a speech before the National Academy of Sciences, President Obama put forth a goal of increasing the national investment in R&D to more than 3% of the U.S. gross domestic product (GDP), but did not provide details on how this goal might be achieved.

Despite the continuing debate on what is the appropriate role of government and what constitutes a suitable government technology development policy, it remains an undisputed fact that what the government does or does not do affects the private sector and the marketplace. The various rules, regulations, and other activities of the government have become de facto policy as they relate to, and affect, innovation and technological advancement.

LEGISLATIVE INITIATIVES AND CURRENT PROGRAMS

Legislative initiatives have reflected a trend toward expanding the government's role beyond traditional funding of mission-oriented R&D and basic research toward the facilitation of technological advancement to meet other critical national needs, including the economic growth that flows from new commercialization and use of technologies and techniques in the private sector. An overview of congressional legislation shows federal efforts aimed at (1) encouraging industry to spend more on R&D; (2) assisting small high-technology businesses; (3) promoting joint research activities between companies; (4) fostering cooperative work between industry and universities; (5) facilitating the transfer of technology from the federal laboratories to the private sector; and (6) providing incentives for quality improvements. These initiatives tend toward removing barriers to technology development in the private sector (thereby permitting market forces to operate) and providing incentives to encourage increased private sector R&D activities. While most focus primarily on research, some also involve policies and programs associated with technology development and commercialization.

Increased R&D Spending

To foster research in the private sector, Congress created a temporary tax credit for incremental increases in qualified research spending. The 1981 Economic Recovery Tax Act (P.L. 97-34) provided a 25% tax credit for the increase in a firm's qualified research costs above the average expenditures for the previous three tax years. Qualified costs included in-house expenditures such as wages for researchers, material costs, and payments for use of equipment; 65% of corporate grants towards basic research at universities and other relevant institutions; and 65% of payments for contract research. The credit applied to research expenditures through 1985. While never made permanent, the Research and Experimentation Tax Credit has been extended many times. Several changes have been made to the rate and to the definition of qualified expenses. Most recently, the credit expired at the end of calendar year 2011.[3]

In 1982, the Small Business Development Act (P.L. 97-219) established Small Business Innovation Research (SBIR) programs within the major federal R&D agencies designed to increase participation of small, innovative companies in federally funded research and development.[4] Extended several times, the program requires that a set percentage of each agency's applicable extramural R&D budget is to be used to support mission-related work in small companies. Funding is, in part, dependent on companies obtaining private sector support for the commercialization of the resulting products or processes. The program had been reauthorized through September 30, 2017. Based on the success of the SBIR initiative, a pilot effort, the Small Business Technology Transfer (STTR) program, was created in 1992 to encourage firms to work with universities or federal laboratories to commercialize the results of basic research performed within these institutions. Also funded by a set-aside, the STTR program has been reauthorized several times and is currently scheduled to sunset on September 30, 2017.

The Omnibus Trade and Competitiveness Act of 1988 (P.L. 100-418) created the Advanced Technology Program (ATP) at the Department of Commerce's National Institute of Standards and Technology (NIST).[5] ATP provided seed funding, matched by private sector investment, for companies or consortia of universities, industries, and/or government laboratories to accelerate development of generic technologies with broad application across industries. The first awards were made in 1991. As of the end of 2007, when ATP was terminated and replaced by the Technology Innovation Program, 824 projects had been funded representing approximately $1.6 billion in federal dollars matched by $1.5 billion in private sector financing. About 68% of the awardees were small businesses or cooperative efforts led by such firms; 227 projects were joint ventures.[6]

The Technology Innovation Program was created by P.L. 110-69, the America COMPETES Act.[7] Until funding for the program ended in FY2012, TIP was similar to ATP in the intent to promote high-risk R&D that would be of broad-based economic benefit to the nation. However, there were several differences in the operation of the new activity. Awards under TIP were limited to small and medium-sized businesses whereas grants under ATP were available to companies regardless of size. In addition, in the Advanced Technology Program, joint ventures were required to include two separately owned for-profit firms and could include universities, government laboratories, and other research establishments as participants in the project but not as recipients of the grant. In the TIP initiative, a joint venture could involve two separately owned for-profit companies but could also have been comprised of one small or medium-sized firm and a university (or other non-profit research organization). A single company could receive up to $2 million for up to three years under ATP; under TIP, the participating company (which must be a small or medium-sized business) could have received up to $3 million for up to three years. In ATP, small and medium-sized companies were not required to cost share (large firms provided 60% of the total cost of the project), while in TIP there was a 50% cost sharing requirement which, again, only applied to the small and medium-sized businesses that are eligible. There were no funding limits for the five- year funding available for joint ventures under ATP; the TIP limited joint venture funding to $9 million for up to five years. The Advisory Board that was created to assist in the Advanced Technology Program included industry representatives as well as federal government personnel and representatives from other research organizations. The Advisory Board for the Technology Innovation Program was comprised of only private sector members.

In January 2009, nine awards were announced for "new research projects to develop advanced sensing technologies that would enable timely and detailed monitoring and inspection of the structural health of bridges, roadways and water systems that comprise a significant component of the nation's public infrastructure." According to TIP, $42.5 million in federal money was expected to be matched by $45.7 million in private sector support. Twenty more awards were announced in December 2009 totaling almost $71.0 million in NIST financing with approximately $145.7 million in funding from other sources. Of the projects selected for the two solicitations, thirteen were in the area of monitoring and inspection of civil infrastructure; four were in the area of advanced repair of civil infrastructure; eleven were in the area of process scale up for advanced materials; and one was in the area of predictive modeling for advanced materials. Nine additional projects in various areas including biopharmaceuticals, electronics, nanotechnology, renewable energy, and energy sources received awards of more than $22 million in December 2010. Federal funding for these projects was expected to be matched by approximately $24 million in private sector support.[8]

According to NIST, no new TIP awards were made in FY2011. The $44.8 million appropriated for the program in P.L. 112-10 was used for the continued support of ongoing TIP and ATP projects.[9] No FY2012 funds were appropriated for TIP.

Industry-University Cooperative Efforts

The promotion of cooperative efforts among academia and industry is aimed at increasing the potential for the commercialization of technology.[10] Traditionally, basic research has been performed in universities or in the federal laboratory system while the business community focuses on the manufacture or provision of products, processes, or services. Universities are especially suited to undertake basic research. Their mission is to educate and basic research is an integral part of the educational process. Universities generally are able to perform these activities because they do not have to produce goods for the marketplace and therefore can do research not necessarily tied to the development of a commercial product or process.

Subsequent to World War II, the federal government supplanted industry as the primary source of funding for basic research in universities. It also became the principal determinant of the type and direction of the research performed in academia. This resulted in a disconnect between the university and industrial communities. The separation and isolation of the parties involved in the innovation process is thought by many observers to be a barrier to technological progress. The difficulties in moving an idea from the concept stage to a commercial product or process may be compounded when several entities are involved. Legislation to stimulate cooperative efforts among those involved in technology development has been viewed as one way to promote innovation and facilitate the international competitiveness of U.S. industry.

Several laws have attempted to encourage industry-university cooperation. Title II of the Economic Recovery Tax Act of 1981 (P.L. 97-34) provided, in part, a 25% tax credit for 65% of all company payments to universities for the performance of basic research.[11] Firms were also permitted a larger tax deduction for charitable contributions of equipment used in scientific research at academic institutions. The Tax Reform Act of 1986 (P.L. 99-514) kept this latter provision, but reduced the credit for university basic research to 20% of all corporate expenditures for this over the sum of a fixed research floor plus any decrease in non-research giving.

The 1981 act also provided an increased charitable deduction for donations of new equipment by a manufacturer to an institution of higher education. This equipment must be used for research or research training for physical or biological sciences within the United States. The tax deduction is equal to the manufacturer's cost plus one-half the difference between the manufacturer's cost and the market value, as long as it does not exceed twice the cost basis. Extended numerous times, with certain changes, the research and experimentation tax credit expired at the end of calendar year 2011.

An additional legislative initiative to foster interaction between academia and the business community is contained in amendments to the patent and trademark laws, commonly referred to as the "Bayh-Dole Act."[12] This law is intended to use patent ownership as an incentive for private sector development and commercialization of federally supported R&D. Title to inventions made by contractors receiving federal research funds is to be vested in the contractor if they are small businesses, universities, or not-for-profit institutions. Certain rights to the patent are reserved for the government and these organizations are required to commercialize within a predetermined and agreed upon time frame. Providing universities with patent title is expected to encourage licensing to industry where the technology can be manufactured or used thereby creating a financial return to the academic institution. University patent applications and licensing have increased significantly since this law was enacted.

Subsequently, the CREATE Act, P.L. 108-453, made changes in the patent laws to further promote cooperative research and development among universities, government, and the private sector. The bill amends Section 103(c) of title 25, United States Code, such that certain actions between researchers under a joint research agreement will not preclude patentability.[13]

Joint Industrial Research

Private sector investments in basic research are often costly, long term, and risky. Although not all advances in technology are the result of research, it is often the foundation of important new innovations. To encourage increased industrial involvement in research, legislation was enacted to allow for joint ventures in this arena. It is argued that cooperative research reduces risks and costs and allows for work to be performed that crosses traditional boundaries of expertise and experience. Such collaborative efforts make use of existing and support the development of new resources, facilities, knowledge, and skills.

The National Cooperative Research Act (P.L. 98-462) encourages companies to undertake joint research. The legislation clarifies the antitrust laws and requires that a "rule of reason" standard be applied in determinations of violations of these laws; cooperative research ventures are not to be judged illegal "per se." It eliminates treble damage awards for those research ventures found in violation of the antitrust laws if prior disclosure (as defined in the law) has been made. P.L. 98-462 also makes changes in the way attorney fees are awarded. Defendants can collect attorney fees in specified circumstances, including when the claim is judged frivolous, unreasonable, without foundation, or made in bad faith. However, the attorney fee award to the prevailing party may be offset if the court decides that the prevailing party conducted a portion of the litigation in a manner which was frivolous, unreasonable, without foundation, or in bad faith. These provisions were included to discourage frivolous litigation against joint research ventures without simultaneously discouraging suits of plaintiffs with valid claims. Between 1985 (when the law went into effect) and August 2009, 1,343 joint ventures have filed with the Justice Department.[14]

P.L. 103-42, the National Cooperative Production Amendments Act of 1993, amended the National Cooperative Research Act by, among other things, extending the original law's provisions to joint manufacturing ventures. These provisions are only applicable, however, to cooperative production when (1) the principal manufacturing facilities are "located in the United States or its territories, and (2) each person who controls any party to such venture ... is a United States person, or a foreign person from a country whose law accords antitrust treatment no less favorable to United States persons than to such country's domestic persons with respect to participation in joint ventures for production."

Commercialization of the Results of Federally Funded R&D

Another approach to encouraging the commercialization of technology involves the transfer of technology from federal laboratories and contractors to the private sector where commercialization can proceed. Because the federal laboratory system has extensive science and technology resources and expertise developed in pursuit of mission responsibilities, it is a potential source of new ideas and knowledge which may be used in the business community.[15]

At the time legislation relating to technology transfer was considered by Congress in the late 1970s, the commercialization level of the results of federally funded R&D remained low despite the potential offered by the resources of the federal laboratory system. Studies indicated that only approximately 10% of federally owned patents were ever utilized. There were many reasons for this low level of usage, one of which is the fact that some technologies and/or patents have no market application. However, industry unfamiliarity with these technologies, the "not-invented- here" syndrome, and perhaps more significantly, the ambiguities associated with obtaining title to or exclusive license to federally owned patents also contribute to the low level of commercialization.

Over the years, several governmental efforts have been undertaken to augment industry's awareness of federal R&D resources. The Federal Laboratory Consortium for Technology Transfer was created in 1972 (from a Department of Defense program) to assist in moving technology from the federal government to state and local governments and the private sector. To expand on the work of the Federal Laboratory Consortium, and to provide added emphasis on the commercialization of government technology, Congress passed P.L. 96-480, the Stevenson-Wydler Technology Innovation Act of 1980. Prior to this law, technology transfer was not an explicit mandate of the federal departments and agencies with the exception of the National Aeronautics and Space Administration. To provide "legitimacy" to the numerous technology activities of the government, Congress, with strong bipartisan support, enacted P.L. 96-480 which explicitly states that the federal government has the responsibility, "to ensure the full use of the results of the nation's federal investment in research and development." Section 11 of the law created a system within the federal government to identify and disseminate information and expertise on what technologies or techniques are available for transfer. Offices of Research and Technology Applications were established in each federal laboratory to distinguish technologies and ideas with potential applications in other settings.

Several amendments to the Stevenson-Wydler Technology Innovation Act have been enacted to provide additional incentives for the commercialization of technology. P.L. 99-502, the Federal Technology Transfer Act, authorizes activities designed to encourage industry, universities, and federal laboratories to work cooperatively. It also establishes incentives for federal laboratory employees to promote the commercialization of the results of federally funded research and development. The law amends P.L. 96-480 to allow government-owned, government-operated laboratories to enter into cooperative R&D agreements (CRADAs) with universities and the private sector. This authority is extended to government-owned, contractor-operated laboratories by the Department of Defense FY1990 Authorization Act, P.L. 101-189.[16] Companies, regardless of size, may be allowed to retain title to inventions resulting from research performed under cooperative agreements. The federal government retains a royalty-free license to use these patents. The Technology Transfer Improvements and Advancement Act (P.L. 104-113), clarifies the dispensation of intellectual property rights under CRADAs to facilitate the implementation of these cooperative efforts. The Federal Laboratory Consortium is given a legislative mandate to assist in the coordination of technology transfer. To further promote the use of the results of federal R&D,

certain agencies are mandated to create a cash awards program and a royalty sharing activity for federal scientists, engineers, and technicians in recognition of efforts toward commercialization of this federally developed technology. These efforts are facilitated by a provision of the National Defense Authorization Act for FY1991 (P.L. 101-510), which amends the Stevenson-Wydler Technology Innovation Act to allow government agencies and laboratories to develop partnership intermediary programs to augment the transfer of laboratory technology to the small business sector.

Amendments to the Patent and Trademark law contained in Title V of P.L. 98-620 made changes which are designed to improve the transfer of technology from the federal laboratories— especially those operated by contractors—to the private sector and increase the chances of successful commercialization of these technologies. This law permits the contractor at government-owned, contractor-operated laboratories (GOCOs) to make decisions at the laboratory level as to the granting of licenses for subject inventions. This increased the potential for effecting greater interaction between laboratories and industry in the transfer of technology. Royalties on these inventions are also permitted to go back to the laboratory contractor to be used for additional R&D, awards to individual laboratory inventors, or education. While there is a cap on the amount of the royalty returning directly to the lab in order not to disrupt the agency's mission requirements and congressionally mandated R&D agenda, the establishment of discretionary funds gives contractor-operated laboratories added incentive to encourage technology transfer.

Under P.L. 98-620, private companies, regardless of size, are allowed to obtain exclusive licenses for the life of the patent. Prior restrictions allowed large firms use of exclusive license for only 5 of the 17 years (now 20 years) of the life of the patent. This was expected to encourage improved technology transfer from the federal laboratories or the universities (in the case of university operated GOCOs) to large corporations which often have the resources necessary for development and commercialization activities. In addition, the law permits GOCOs (those operated by universities or nonprofit institutions) to retain title to inventions made in the laboratory within certain defined limitations. Those laboratories operated by large companies are not included in this provision.

P.L. 106-404, the Technology Transfer Commercialization Act, altered practices concerning patents held by the government to make it easier for federal agencies to license such inventions. The law amends the Stevenson-Wydler Technology Innovation Act and the Bayh-Dole Act to decrease the time delays associated with obtaining an exclusive or partially exclusive license. Previously, agencies were required to publicize the availability of technologies for three months using the *Federal Register* and then provide an additional 60 day notice of intent to license by an interested company. Under this legislation, the time period was shortened to 15 days in recognition of the ability of the internet to offer widespread notification and the necessity of time constraints faced by industry in commercialization activities. Certain rights are retained by the government. The bill also allows licenses for existing government-owned inventions to be included in CRADAs.

The Omnibus Trade and Competitiveness Act created a program of regional centers to assist small manufacturing companies use knowledge and technologies developed in the government research establishment.[17] Federal funding for the centers is matched by non-federal sources including state and local governments and industry. Originally, seven Regional Centers for the Transfer of Manufacturing Technology were selected. The initial program was expanded in 1994 to create the Manufacturing Extension Partnership (MEP) to meet new and growing needs of the community. In a more varied approach, the Partnership involves both large centers and smaller, more dispersed affiliated organizations. Centers now operate in all 50 states and Puerto Rico. Since the manufacturing extension activity was created in 1989, awards made by NIST have resulted in the creation of approximately 400 regional offices. [It should be noted that the Department of Defense also funded 36 centers through its Technology Reinvestment Project (TRP) in FY1994 and FY1995. When the TRP was terminated, NIST took over support for 20 of these programs in FY1996 and funded the remaining efforts during FY1997.]

A new NIST program of partnerships between industry and other educational or research institutions to develop new manufacturing processes, techniques, or materials was authorized (but not funded) by the American COMPETES Act. In addition, the COMPETES Act authorized a manufacturing fellowship program with stipends available for post-doctoral work at NIST that has not been instituted to date.

In October 2010, NIST announced the award of $9.1 million in cooperative agreements for 22 projects "designed to enhance the productivity, technological performance and global competitiveness of U.S. manufacturers."[18] The funding was granted on a competitive basis to non-profit organizations that will work with the MEP centers and address one or more of the areas that have been identified by NIST as critical to U.S. manufacturing. These activities differ from the established MEP effort in which no new manufacturing research is conducted and funded as existing manufacturing technology is applied to the needs of small and medium-sized firms.

A Different Approach?

As indicated above, the laws affecting the R&D environment have included both direct and indirect measures to facilitate technological innovation. In general, direct measures are those which involve budget outlays and the provision of services by government agencies. Indirect measures include financial incentives and legal changes (e.g., liability or regulatory reform; new antitrust arrangements). Supporters of indirect approaches argue that the market is superior to government in deciding which technologies are worthy of investment. Mechanisms that enhance the market's opportunities and abilities to make such choices are preferred. Advocates further state that dependency on agency discretion to assist one technology in preference to another will inevitably be subjected to political pressures from entrenched interests. Proponents of direct government assistance maintain, conversely, that indirect methods can be wasteful and ineffective and that they can compromise other goals of public policy in the hope of stimulating innovative performance. Advocates of direct approaches argue that it is important to put the country's scarce resources to work on those technologies that have the greatest promise as determined by industry and supported by its willingness to match federal funding.

In the past, participants in the debates generally did not make definite (or exclusionary) choices between the two approaches, nor consistently favor one over the other. For example, some proponents of a stronger direct role for the government in innovation also have supported enhanced tax preferences for R&D spending, an indirect mechanism. Opponents of direct federal funding for specific projects may have nevertheless backed similar activities focused on more general areas such as manufacturing or information technology. However, in recent congresses, legislators directed many of their efforts toward eliminating or curtailing some of the programs that previously had enjoyed bipartisan support. Initiatives to terminate the Advanced Technology Program and the Technology Innovation Program reflected concern over the role of government in developing commercial technologies. While appropriations for several programs decreased, and both ATP and TIP are no longer funded, support for several ongoing activities has continued. How the debate over federal funding evolves in the Congress may serve to redefine thinking about the government's efforts in promoting technological advancement in the private sector.

End Notes

[1] Edwin Mansfield, "Social Returns From R&D: Findings, Methods, and Limitations," *Research/Technology Management*, November-December 1991, 24. See also Charles I. Jones and John C. Williams, "Measuring the Social Return to R&D," *Quarterly Journal of Economics*, November 1998, 1119 and Richard R. Nelson and Paul M. Romer, "Science, Economic Growth, and Public Policy," in Bruce R. Smith and Claude E. Barfield, eds. *Technology, R&D, and the Economy*, (Washington, The Brookings Institution and the American Enterprise Institute, Washington, 1996), 57.

[2] Available from author.

[3] CRS Report RL31181, *Research Tax Credit: Current Law, Legislation in the 112th Congress, and Policy Issues*, by Gary Guenther.

[4] See CRS Report 96-402, *Small Business Innovation Research (SBIR) Program*, by Wendy H. Schacht, and CRS Report RS22865, *The Small Business Innovation Research (SBIR) Program: Reauthorization Efforts*, by Wendy H. Schacht.

[5] See CRS Report 95-36, *The Advanced Technology Program*, by Wendy H. Schacht.

[6] National Institute of Standards and Technology, "Historical Statistics on ATP Awards/Winners," available at http://www.atp.nist.gov/eao/statisticshtm.

[7] See CRS Report RS22815, *The Technology Innovation Program*, by Wendy H. Schacht.

[8] National Institute of Standards and Technology, "NIST Announces $22 Million in Funding for Advanced Manufacturing Research in Electronics, Biotechnology and Nanotechnology," December 15, 2010, available at http://www.nist.gov/tip/tip_121510.cfm.

[9] See http://www.nist.gov/tip/.

[10] For more information see CRS Report RL33526, *Cooperative R&D: Federal Efforts to Promote Industrial Competitiveness*, by Wendy H. Schacht.

[11] See CRS Report RL31181, *Research Tax Credit: Current Law, Legislation in the 112th Congress, and Policy Issues*, by Gary Guenther.

[12] See CRS Report RL32076, *The Bayh-Dole Act: Selected Issues in Patent Policy and the Commercialization of Technology*, by Wendy H. Schacht and CRS Report RL30320, *Patent Ownership and Federal Research and Development (R&D): A Discussion on the Bayh-Dole Act and the Stevenson-Wydler Act*, by Wendy H. Schacht.

[13] See CRS Report RS21882, *Collaborative R&D and the Cooperative Research and Technology Enhancement (CREATE) Act*, by Wendy H. Schacht.

[14] Dean V. Williamson, How do Research Joint Ventures Exploit Government R&D Program?: Evidence from the National Cooperative Research Act, the Advanced Technology Program, and the Department of Defense, Preliminary study, June 2010, 6, available at http://extranet.isnie.org/uploads/isnie2010/williamson.pdf.

[15] See CRS Report RL33527, *Technology Transfer: Use of Federally Funded Research and Development*, by Wendy H. Schacht.

[16] See CRS Report 95-150, *Cooperative Research and Development Agreements (CRADAs)*, by Wendy H. Schacht.

[17] See CRS Report 97-104, *Manufacturing Extension Partnership Program: An Overview*, by Wendy H. Schacht.

[18] National Institute of Standards and Technology, NIST Manufacturing Extension Partnership Awards $9.1 Million for 22 Projects to Enhance U.S. Manufacturers' Global Competitiveness, Press Release, October 5, 2010, available at http://www.nist.gov/mep/upload/100410-MEP-Competition-press-release-FINAL.pdf.

In: The United States Research Enterprise ISBN: 978-1-62417-916-7
Editor: Daniel S. Rosser

Chapter 3

COOPERATIVE R&D: FEDERAL EFFORTS TO PROMOTE INDUSTRIAL COMPETITIVENESS*

Wendy H. Schacht

SUMMARY

In response to the foreign challenge in the global marketplace, the United States Congress has explored ways to stimulate technological advancement in the private sector. The government has supported various efforts to promote cooperative research and development activities among industry, universities, and the federal R&D establishment designed to increase the competitiveness of American industry and to encourage the generation of new products, processes, and services.

Collaborative ventures are intended to accommodate the strengths and responsibilities of all sectors involved in innovation and technology development. Academia, industry, and government often have complementary functions. Joint projects allow for the sharing of costs, risks, facilities, and expertise.

Cooperative activity covers various institutional and legal arrangements including industry- industry, industry-university, and industry-government efforts. Proponents of joint ventures argue that they permit work to be done that is too expensive for one company to support and allow for R&D that

* This is an edited, reformatted and augmented version of the Congressional Research Service Publication, CRS Report for Congress RL33526, dated December 3, 2012.

crosses traditional boundaries of expertise and experience. Such arrangements make use of existing, and support the development of new, resources, facilities, knowledge, and skills. Opponents argue that these endeavors dampen competition necessary for innovation.

Federal efforts to encourage cooperative activities include the National Cooperative Research Act; the National Cooperative Production Act; tax changes permitting credits for industry payments to universities for R&D and deductions for contributions of equipment used in academic research; and amendments to the patent laws vesting title to inventions made under federal funding in universities. Technology transfer from the government to the private sector is facilitated by several laws. In addition, there are various ongoing cooperative programs supported by multiple federal departments and agencies.

Given the increased popularity of cooperative programs, questions might be raised as to whether they are meeting expectations. Among the issues before Congress are whether joint ventures contribute to industrial competitiveness and what role, if any, the government has in facilitating such arrangements.

COLLABORATIVE R&D: BACKGROUND AND RATIONALE

In response to concerns over competition from foreign firms, the U.S. Congress has increasingly looked for ways the federal government can stimulate technological innovation in the private sector. This technological advancement is critical in that it contributes to economic growth and long term increases in our standard of living. New technologies can create new industries and new jobs; expand the types and geographic distribution of services; and reduce production costs by making more efficient use of resources. The development and application of technology also plays a major role in determining patterns of international trade by affecting the comparative advantages of industrial sectors. Since technological progress is not necessarily determined by economic conditions, it can have effects on trade independent of shifts in macroeconomic factors that may affect the marketplace.

Joint ventures are an attempt to facilitate technological advancement within the industrial community. Academia, industry, and government can play complementary roles in technology development. While opponents argue that cooperative ventures stifle competition, proponents assert that they are designed to accommodate the strengths and responsibilities of these sectors. Collaborative projects attempt to utilize and integrate what the participants do best and to direct these efforts toward the goal of generating new goods, processes, and services for the marketplace. They allow for shared costs, shared risks, shared facilities, and shared expertise.

The lexicon of current cooperative activity covers various different institutional and legal arrangements. These ventures might include industry-industry joint projects involving the creation of a new entity to undertake research, the reassignment of researchers to a new effort, and/or hiring new personnel. Collaborative industry-university efforts may revolve around activities in which industry supports centers (sometimes cross-disciplinary) for research at universities, funds individual research projects, and/or exchanges personnel. Cooperative activities with the federal government might include projects that use federal facilities and researchers, federal funding for industry-industry or industry-university efforts, or financial support for centers of excellence at universities to which the private sector has access.

There are many different types of cooperative arrangements. The flexibility associated with this concept can allow for the development of institutional and organizational plans tailored to the specific needs of the particular project. Issues of patent ownership, disclosure of information, licensing, and antitrust are to be resolved on an individual basis within the general guidelines established by law governing joint ventures.

Collaborative ventures can be structured either "horizontally" or "vertically." The former involves efforts in which companies work together to perform research and then use the results of this research within their individual organizations. The latter involves activities where researchers, producers, and users work together. Both approaches are seen as ways to address some of the perceived obstacles to the competitiveness of American firms in the marketplace.

Joint Industrial Research

Traditionally, the federal government has funded research and development (R&D) to meet mission requirements; in areas where the government is the primary user of the results; and/or where there is an identified need for R&D not being performed in the private sector. Most government support is for basic research which is often long-term and highly risky for individual companies; yet research can be the foundation for breakthrough achievements which can revolutionize the marketplace. Studies have shown that inventions based on R&D are the more important ones. However, the societal benefits of research tend to be greater than those that can be captured by the firm performing the work. Thus the rationale for federal funding of research in industry.

The major emphasis of legislative activity has been on augmenting research in the industrial community. This focus is reflected in efforts to encourage companies to undertake cooperative research arrangements and expand the opportunities available for increases in research activities. Collaboration permits work to be done which is too expensive for one company to fund and also allows for R&D that crosses traditional boundaries of expertise and experience. A joint venture makes use of existing, and supports development of new resources, facilities, knowledge, and skills.

Policy decisions focusing on increased research as a prelude to increased technological advancement were based upon the "pipeline model" of innovation. This process was understood to be a series of distinct steps from an idea through product development, engineering, testing, and commercialization to a marketable product, process, or service. Thus increases at the beginning of the pipeline—in research—were expected to result in analogous increases in innovation at the end. However, this model is no longer considered valid. Innovation is rarely a linear process and new technologies and techniques often occur that do not require basic or applied research or development. Most innovations are actually incremental improvements to existing products and processes. In some areas, particularly biotechnology, research is closer to a commercial product than this conception would indicate. In others, the differentiation between basic and applied research is artificial. The critical factor is the commercialization of the technology. Economic benefits accrue only when a technology or technique is brought to the marketplace where it can be sold to generate income and/or applied to increase productivity.

In the recent past, it was increasingly common to find that foreign companies were commercializing the results of U.S. funded research at a faster pace than American firms. In a rapidly changing technological environment, the speed at which a product, process, or service is brought to the marketplace is often a crucial factor in its competitiveness. The recognition that more than research needs to be done has lead to other approaches at cooperative efforts aimed at expediting the commercialization of the results of the American R&D endeavor. These include industry-university joint activities, use of the federal laboratory system by industry, and industry- industry development efforts where manufacturers, suppliers, and users work together.

Industry-University Cooperative Efforts

Industry-university cooperation in R&D is one important mechanism intended to facilitate technological innovation. Traditionally, universities perform much of the basic research integral to certain technological advancements. They are generally able to undertake fundamental research because it is part of the educational process and because they do not have to produce for the marketplace. The risks attached to work in this setting are fewer than those in industry where companies must earn profits. Universities also educate and train the scientists, engineers, and managers employed by companies.

Academic institutions do not have the commercialization capacity available in industry and necessary to translate the results of research into products and processes that can be sold in the marketplace. Thus, if the work performed in the academic environment is to be integrated into goods and services, a mechanism to link the two sectors must be available. Prior to World War II, industry was the primary source of funding for basic research in universities. This financial support helped shape priorities and build relationships. However, after the war the federal government supplanted industry as the major financial contributor and became the principal determinant of the type and direction of the research performed in academic institutions. This situation resulted in a disconnect between the university and industrial communities. Because industry and not the government is responsible for commercialization, the difficulties in moving an idea from the research stage to a marketable product or process appear to have been compounded.

Efforts to encourage increased collaboration between the academic and industrial sectors might be expected to augment the contribution of both parties to technological advancement. Company support for research within the university provides additional funds and information on the concerns and direction of industry. For many companies, access to expertise and facilities outside of the firm expands or complements available internal resources. Yet, such cooperation should not necessarily be seen as a panacea. Oftentimes, collaborative ventures fail because of various factors including conflicting goals, differing research cultures, and financial disagreements.

Federal Laboratory-Industry Interaction

The federal government can share its extensive facilities, expertise, knowledge, and new technologies with partners in a cooperative venture. In certain cases, the government laboratories have scientists and engineers with experience and skills, as well as equipment, not available elsewhere. The government also has a vested interest in technology development. It does not have the mandate or resources to manufacture goods but has a stake in the availability of products and processes to meet mission requirements. In addition, technological advancement contributes to the economic growth vital to the health and security of the nation.

Collaboration between government laboratories and industry is not, however, just a one way street. In several technological areas, particularly electronics and computer software, the private sector is more advanced in technologies important to the national defense and welfare of this country. Interaction with industry offers federal scientists and engineers valuable information to be used within the government R&D enterprise.

FEDERAL INITIATIVES IN COOPERATIVE R&D

The cooperative venture concept has a long history. In the early 1970s, the National Science Foundation established its Industry-University Cooperative Research Centers program. The Electric Power Research Institute, a research organization supported by the electric power utilities, has been in operation since 1973. In the private sector, the Microelectronics and Computer Technology Corporation which performed research for its member firms prior to its dissolution, and the Semiconductor Research Corporation which funds research in universities, were created in the early 1980s. The difference today is the number of projects and the scope of legislative activity designed to promote cooperative ventures.

Faced with pressures from foreign competition, the government's interest has expanded beyond that of funding R&D, to meeting other critical national needs including the economic growth that flows from new commercialization in the private sector. While acknowledging that the commercialization of technology is the responsibility of the business community, in the past several years the government has attempted to stimulate innovation and technological advancement in industry. These activities often involve the removal of barriers to technology development in the private sector, thereby permitting market forces to operate and the provision of incentives to encourage increased innovation-related efforts in industry. Cooperative R&D efforts are a part of both these trends.

To address competitiveness concerns associated with joint research and to encourage companies to participate in this work which is typically long-term, risky, and often too expensive for one company to finance, Congress passed the National Cooperative Research Act (P.L. 98-462) in 1984. This legislation clarified the antitrust laws and requires that the "rule of reason" standard be applied in determinations of violations of these laws; that cooperative research ventures are not to be judged illegal "per se." It also eliminated treble damage awards for those research ventures found in violation of the antitrust laws if prior disclosure (as defined in the law) has been made. In addition, the act made some changes in the way attorney fees are awarded to discourage frivolous litigation against joint research ventures without simultaneously discouraging suits of plaintiffs with valid claims. Between 1985 (when the law went into effect) and August 2009, 1,343 joint ventures have filed with the Justice Department.[1]

The provisions of the National Cooperative Research Act were extended to joint manufacturing ventures by P.L. 103-42, the National Cooperative Production Amendments Act of 1993. These provisions are only applicable, however, to cooperative production when the principal manufacturing facilities are "located in the United States or its territories, and each person who controls any party to such venture ... is a United States person, or a foreign person from a country whose law accords antitrust treatment no less favorable to United States persons than to such country's domestic persons with respect to participation in joint ventures for production."

Additional collaborative work was facilitated by the Advanced Technology Program (ATP) at the Department of Commerce's National Institute of Standards and Technology which was created by the Omnibus Trade and Competitiveness Act of 1988 (P.L. 100-418).[2] Prior to its replacement in FY2008 by the Technology Innovation Program (which lost funding in FY2012), ATP provided seed funding, matched by private sector investment, to companies or consortia comprised of universities, companies, and/or government laboratories for the development of generic technologies that have broad application across industrial sectors. As of the end of 2007 when the program was terminated, 824 projects had been funded representing approximately $1.6 billion in federal financing matched by $1.5 billion in financing from the private sector.[3] Of these projects, approximately 28% were joint ventures.

The Technology Innovation Program (TIP) replaced ATP but received significantly reduced funding in FY2011 and no support in FY2012.[4] While similar in intent to ATP in that it was designed to promote high-risk R&D that would be of broad-based economic benefit to the Nation, TIP operated somewhat differently yet still encouraged joint ventures. Funding under TIP was limited to small and medium-sized businesses whereas grants under ATP were available to companies regardless of size. In the Advanced Technology Program, joint ventures were required to include two separately owned for-profit firms and could include universities, government laboratories, and other research establishments as participants in the project but not as recipients of the grant. Under TIP, a joint venture could have involved two separately owned for-profit companies but also could be comprised of one small or medium-sized firm and a university. A single company was able to receive up to $2 million for up to three years under ATP; under TIP, the participating company (which must be a small or medium-sized business) could receive up to $3 million for up to three years. In ATP, small and medium-sized companies were not required to cost share (large firms provided 60% of the total cost of the project) while in TIP there was a 50% cost sharing requirement which, again, only applied to the small and medium-sized businesses that were eligible. There were no funding limits for the five-year funding available for joint ventures under ATP; TIP limited joint venture funding to $9 million for up to five years. The Advisory Board that was created to assist in the Advanced Technology Program included industry representatives as well as federal government personnel and representatives from other research organizations. The Advisory Board for the Technology Innovation Program was comprised of only private sector members.

In January 2009, nine awards were announced for "new research projects to develop advanced sensing technologies that would enable timely and detailed monitoring and inspection of the structural health of bridges, roadways and water systems that comprise a significant component of the nation's public infrastructure." According to TIP, $42.5 million in federal money was expected to be matched by $45.7 in private sector support. Twenty more awards were announced in December 2009 totaling almost $71.0 million in NIST financing with approximately $145.7 million in funding from other sources. Of the projects selected for the two solicitations, thirteen were in the area of monitoring and inspection of civil infrastructure; four were in the area of advanced repair of civil infrastructure; eleven were in the area of process scale up for advanced materials; and one was in the area of predictive modeling for advanced materials. Nine additional projects in various areas including biopharmaceuticals, electronics, nanotechnology, renewable energy, and energy sources received awards of more than $22 million in December 2010. Federal funding for these projects was expected to be matched by approximately $24 million in private sector support.[5]

Additional laws have attempted to facilitate industry-university cooperation. Title II of the Economic Recovery Tax Act of 1981 (P.L. 97-34) provided, in part, a temporary 25% tax credit for 65% of all company payments to universities for the performance of basic research.[6] Firms were also permitted a larger tax deduction for charitable contributions of equipment used in scientific research at academic institutions. The Tax Reform Act of 1986 (P.L. 99-514) kept this latter provision, but reduced the credit for university basic research to 20% of all corporate expenditures for this work over the sum of a fixed research floor plus any decrease in non- research giving.

The 1981 Act also provided an increased charitable deduction for donations of new equipment by a manufacturer to an institution of higher education. This equipment must be used for research or training for physical or biological sciences within the United States. The tax deduction was equal to the manufacturer's cost plus one-half the difference between the manufacturer's cost and the market value, as long as it does not exceed twice the cost basis.

While never made permanent, the research tax credit has been extended numerous times and changes have been made to certain provisions. The credit expired at the close of calendar year 2011.

Amendments to the patent and trademark laws contained in P.L. 96-517, commonly referred to as the "Bayh-Dole" Act, also were designed to foster interaction between academia and the business community.[7] This law provides, in part, for title to inventions made by contractors receiving federal R&D funds to be vested in the contractor if it is a university, not-for-profit institution, or a small business. Certain rights to the patent are reserved for the government and these organizations are required to commercialize within a predetermined and agreed upon time frame. Providing universities with patent title is expected to encourage licensing to industry where the technology can be manufactured or utilized, thereby creating a financial return to the academic institution. University patent applications and licensing have increased since this law was enacted.

Many cooperative industry-industry or industry-university programs are supported and/or organized by the federal departments and agencies. These include, but are not limited to, the National Science Foundation's Engineering

Research Centers, the more than 40 Industry- University Cooperative Research Programs, and the Science and Technology Centers. The Department of Defense supports various Centers of Excellence, as does the Federal Aviation Administration.

While most legislative activities are intended to facilitate technological advance across industries, there have been several efforts to provide direct assistance for cooperative ventures in a particular industry. These initiatives are based, in part, on national defense and economic security concerns over specific technologies that are, or are perceived as, potentially critical to a wide range of businesses. Among the joint ventures, funded primarily by the Department of Defense (DOD), have been SEMATECH (a joint private sector semiconductor manufacturing research effort which is now privately financed) and the National Center for Manufacturing Sciences which also receives support from the Department of Energy, the Department of Transportation, and the Environmental Protection Agency. In addition, DOD supports the Software Engineering Institute and the Department of Energy assists in the US Drive initiative that, among other things, encourages joint R&D between federal laboratories and private firms leading to commercialization.

Cooperation between industry and the federal R&D enterprise is another facet of the effort to increase industrial competitiveness through joint ventures. The federal government will have spent an estimated $138.9 billion in FY2012 on research and development to meet the mission requirements of the federal departments and agencies.[8] This has led to many technologies and techniques, as well as to the generation of knowledge and skills, which may have applications beyond their original intent. To foster their development and commercialization in the industrial community, various laws have established institutions and mechanisms to facilitate the movement of ideas and technologies between the public and private sectors.

The Stevenson-Wydler Technology Innovation Act (P.L. 96-480), as amended by the Federal Technology Transfer Act (P.L. 99-502) and the Department of Defense FY1990 Authorizations (P.L. 101-189), provided, in part, a legislative mandate for technology transfer from the federal government to the private sector, established a series of offices in the agencies and/or laboratories to administer transfer efforts, provided incentives for federal laboratory personnel to actively engage in technology transfer, and created new contractual means for industry to work with the laboratories including cooperative research and development agreements (CRADAs). P.L. 104-113, the National Technology Transfer and Advancement Act, addressed existing policy with respect to the dispensation of intellectual property under a

CRADA by amending the Stevenson-Wydler Act. P.L. 106-404, the Technology Transfer Commercialization Act, made changes in existing practices concerning patents held by the government to make it easier for federal agencies to license such inventions to the private sector for commercialization.[9]

To further promote cooperative research and development among universities, government, and the private sector, changes in the patent laws were made by P.L. 108-453. the CREATE Act.[10] The legislation amended section 103(c) of title 25, United States Code, such that certain actions between researchers under a joint research agreement will not preclude patentability.

A program of regional Centers for the Transfer of Manufacturing Technology (now part of the Hollings Manufacturing Extension Partnership effort) to facilitate the movement to the private sector of knowledge and technologies developed under the aegis of the National Institute of Standards and Technology was established by the Omnibus Trade and Competitiveness Act.[11] In addition, the law required that NIST provide technical assistance to state technology extension programs in an effort to improve private sector access to federal technology. Government- industry collaboration is further encouraged by a provision of the FY1991 National Defense Authorization Act (P.L. 101-510) that amends the Stevenson-Wydler Act to allow government agencies and laboratories to develop partnership intermediary programs to augment the transfer of laboratory technology to the small business community.[12]

Cooperative work between small companies and federal laboratories leading to the commercialization of new technology is the intent of the Small Business Technology Transfer (STTR) program. Created by the Small Business Development Act of 1992, this effort provides funding for research proposals that are developed and executed collaboratively between a small firms and a scientist in a research organization. Extended several times, the program was scheduled to sunset at the end of FY2009, but was temporarily extended several times and is currently scheduled to terminate on September 30, 2017.[13]

ISSUES

It is not yet known whether federal support of cooperative ventures signals a long-term commitment to the development of technology. However, given current concerns over the federal budget, it is unlikely that large sums of government money will be forthcoming for such efforts in the future. Yet, other actions may reflect federal interest in the process of technological advancement. The use of the extensive government R&D system, with its expensive state-of-the- art facilities, can provide both academia and industry with resources that may be beyond their financial ability. And despite the often short-term focus of budget decisions, federal funds and non-monetary contributions to cooperative ventures may be leveraged by contributions from state and local agencies and the private sector.

If the proliferation of programs is any indication, state and local jurisdictions have been in the forefront of cooperative endeavors. Many state and local economic development activities focus on increasing innovation and the use of technology in the private sector. Instead of competing for companies to relocate, many of these jurisdictions now see additional benefits accruing from the creation of new firms and the modernization of existing ones through the application of new technology. Various states and localities are attempting to foster an entrepreneurial climate by undertaking the development and support of a variety of programs to assist existing high technology businesses, to promote the establishment of new companies, and to facilitate the use of new technologies and processes in traditional industries. While these efforts vary by state and locality, many of them include industry-university-government cooperation. Several congressional proposals for increasing cooperative ventures built upon existing state and local activities in these areas.

Proponents of cooperative work argue that certain benefits are associated with joint ventures. The increased popularity of this concept, and expanding federal support for this approach, however, might suggest some questions be raised to assess whether cooperative ventures are meeting expectations. It might be expected that an increasing number of industries and/or companies will come to the federal government for assistance in supporting cooperative R&D activities. Despite opposition by some to what has been described as "picking winners or losers," various sectors of the government have chosen to provide funding for cooperative ventures in specific industries while requiring that the private sector generate matching funds. At the same time, there are programs and policies that attempt to facilitate cooperative efforts across industry in general. Decisions might need to be made whether one approach is better than the other, or if both should continue.

If part of government policy is to respond to individual industry requests for assistance, Congress may opt to consider developing procedures to select between industries and/or companies competing for limited federal funds. Can, and should, federal guidelines be established? In addition, is it possible to determine at this time what type of cooperative ventures are the most effective and efficient? Is there, in fact, one best model or should each venture be tailored to the specific situation? And finally, what are the implications of these decisions for policymaking in Congress?

Development

As noted above, innovation is a dynamic process that can involve idea origination, research, development, commercialization, and diffusion throughout the economy. However, it is not a linear process and an innovation may occur without developing through these steps. In fact, many innovations are incremental changes in existing goods and services in response to unmet market needs. The most crucial factor is the availability or use of the technology or technique in the marketplace.

In the recent past, the commercialization and diffusion of products and processes often stood out as significant problems in terms of the ability of U.S. industries to compete. Firms in several other countries, first Japan and now China, India, and the East Asian newly industrializing countries, have been successful in commercializing the results of R&D. In various instances, this was research initially performed in the United States, as evidenced by the VCR and semiconductor chips. Basic research and the pursuit of science are done successfully in the United States as indicated, in part, by the number of Nobel prizes awarded to Americans. However, excellence in science does not necessarily assure leadership in world markets. It has been noted that the United States was the world's premiere economic power in the 1920s when this nation was far from being in the forefront of science. Instead, market leadership is significantly affected by the development and application of technology to make the goods and services the consumers want to purchase.

Thus, questions may be raised as to whether programs and policies encouraging increased cooperative research, without concomitant efforts to facilitate the development and commercialization of technologies and techniques, can be effective mechanisms to increase the competitiveness of American industry. Do we need to know more about how to encourage the application of the research resulting from joint ventures in the manufacture of products and processes and in the delivery of services? Do these cooperative activities include mechanisms to facilitate the effective and timely transfer of the results back to the companies where they can be developed into goods for the marketplace? Since the major portion of the costs associated with bringing out a new product occur at the development and marketing stages, not in the research phase, should there be additional government incentives to encourage companies to spend funds for commercialization in addition to research?

Manufacturing

It is in the manufacturing arena where American companies appear to be the most vulnerable to foreign competition. Process technologies (those used in manufacturing) can significantly lower the costs of production and increase the quality of goods and services. In *Global Competition*, the President's Commission on Industrial Competitiveness (under former President Reagan) concluded that "... competitive success in many industries today is as much a matter of mastering the most advanced manufacturing processes as it is in pioneering new products."

The costs associated with the development and purchase of new manufacturing equipment are high. This is particularly true for the 350,000 small companies which make up a major segment of the manufacturing community. Several of the cooperative efforts supported by the federal government address these manufacturing concerns. The Manufacturing Technology program of the Department of Defense, the advanced manufacturing initiatives in the Department of Energy, and the Manufacturing Extension Centers operated by the National Institute of Standards and Technology, although all different, are examples of government activities devoted to facilitating the development of new manufacturing techniques and/or their use in industry.

Considering the importance of manufacturing, the existing cooperative programs may not be sufficient to increase the competitiveness of American industry. Are there more effective types of joint ventures? Cooperative efforts, where resources could be pooled and the equipment shared, may be one way to improve the manufacturing capability of U.S. firms, large or small. Will joint manufacturing prove to be a viable option? Should existing cooperative manufacturing programs in certain agencies be expanded or should new efforts in other departments be developed? Should one government agency have the lead in policy determinations; if so, the question remains in which federal department should the responsibility be vested?

Defense vs. Civilian Support

Many of the industries interested in cooperative ventures with federal financial support have approached the Department of Defense and, to a lesser extent, the Department of Energy's Defense Programs because these agencies have the greatest amount of available resources and/or funding. They also tend to have the expertise to operate large-scale programs and maintain close ties with certain industrial sectors which could be encouraged to increase cooperation. In addition, both DOD and DOE have a vested interest in the availability of certain technologies which could be provided by a healthy domestic commercial market. However, questions remain whether sponsorship of certain cooperative ventures by DOD and the Department of Energy's defense-related programs will lead to increased commercialization in the civilian marketplace.

Critics argue that defense spending is not an effective mechanism to increase industry's ability to innovate and develop new technologies. Much of the research and development in the defense arena may be too specialized, overdesigned, and/or too costly to have value for commercial markets. The R&D also tends to concentrate on weapon systems and other defense hardware rather than on process technologies that are often necessary to improve manufacturing productivity. One reason cited for the competitive problems of the machine tool industry was its focus on defense needs rather than on the commercial market which is larger in the aggregate.

On the other hand, the U.S. commitment to military R&D has contributed to a favorable balance of trade in the defense and aerospace industries. In the SEMATECH effort, the purpose of DOD support was to facilitate the *commercial* development of technologies with critical defense applications. The companies involved in SEMATECH were experienced semiconductor manufacturers and were knowledgeable about the markets' needs and operations. Thus, although the initial work performed by this semiconductor consortium may have been partially funded by the Defense Advanced Research Project Agency, it was designed to result in new products and processes in the civilian marketplace where both defense and commercial demand can be met. SEMATECH now operates without direct federal financing.

The issue of cooperative work between the Defense Department and the private sector leading to commercial technologies was addressed in the former Technology Reinvestment Project and was part of the more recent Dual-Use Partnership Project. The Department of Energy has been expanding cooperative R&D activities in defense program laboratories in conjunction with an increase in all DOE collaborative efforts with industry. Decreased technology transfer budgets may impeded this effort, but several DOE defense laboratories are actively pursuing joint ventures with industry.

Access by Foreign Firms

With worldwide communications systems, it is virtually impossible to prevent the flow of scientific and technical information. What is critical to competitiveness is the speed at which this knowledge is used to make products, processes, and services for the marketplace. However, it appears that many foreign firms are willing and able to take the results of research performed both in the United States and their own countries and rapidly make high quality commercial goods. Many of these companies are purchasing American businesses or establishing U.S. subsidiaries to access American expertise. With the increased activity in research consortia, particularly those with federal support, questions might be asked as to whether or not foreign companies should or could be barred from access to the results. A larger issue is how to define an "American company." Is it determined by majority ownership, manufacturing, location, value added to the U.S. economy, or by some other definition? In addition, since technology is most effectively transferred by person-to-person interaction, would cooperative activities between American industry and foreign firms produce an outflow of information which could be used to increase competitive pressures?

Direct vs. Indirect Support

Government efforts to facilitate cooperative ventures have included both indirect supports and direct federal funding. Indirect measures include such things as tax policies, intellectual property rights, and antitrust laws that create incentives for the private sector. Other initiatives included government financing (on a cost shared basis) of joint efforts such as the now terminated Advanced Technology Program and the Technology Innovation Program at the National Institute of Standards and Technology, U.S. Department of Commerce. The Manufacturing Extension Partnership program requires state and/or local matching funds. In the past, participants in the legislative process generally did not make definite (or exclusionary) choices between these two approaches. However, recently these activities have been revisited. For example, efforts to eliminate the Advanced Technology Program and the Technology Innovation Program, funding for flat panel displays, and agricultural extension reflected concern over the role of government in developing commercial technologies and generally resulted in reductions of direct federal financing for such public-private partnerships or their elimination. It remains to be seen what approach will be taken by the Congress as it makes budget decisions that may affect the future of cooperative R&D.

End Notes

[1] Dean V. Williamson, How do Research Joint Ventures Exploit Government R&D Program?: Evidence from the National Cooperative Research Act, the Advanced Technology Program, and the Department of Defense, Preliminary study, June 2010, 6, available at http://extranet.isnie.org/uploads/isnie2010/williamson.pdf.

[2] See CRS Report 95-36, *The Advanced Technology Program*, by Wendy H. Schacht.

[3] National Institute of Standards and Technology, *Historical Statistics on ATP Awards/Winners*, available at http://www.atp.nist.gov/eao/statistics

[4] See CRS Report RS22815, *The Technology Innovation Program*, by Wendy H. Schacht.

[5] National Institute of Standards and Technology, NIST Announces $22 Million in Funding for Advanced Manufacturing Research in Electronics, Biotechnology and Nanotechnology, December 15, 2010, available at http://www.nist.gov/tip/tip_121510.cfm.

[6] See CRS Report RL31181, *Research Tax Credit: Current Law, Legislation in the 112th Congress, and Policy Issues*, by Gary Guenther.

[7] See CRS Report RL32076, *The Bayh-Dole Act: Selected Issues in Patent Policy and the Commercialization of Technology*, by Wendy H. Schacht and CRS Report RL30320, *Patent Ownership and Federal Research and Development (R&D): A Discussion on the Bayh-Dole Act and the Stevenson-Wydler Act*, by Wendy H. Schacht.

[8] Office of Management and Budget, Fiscal Year 2013 Analytical Perspectives, Budget of the U.S. Government, 370, available at http://www.whitehouse.gov/sites/default/files/omb/budget/fy2013/assets/spec.pdf.

[9] See CRS Report RL33527, *Technology Transfer: Use of Federally Funded Research and Development*, by Wendy H. Schacht.

[10] See CRS Report RS21882, *Collaborative R&D and the Cooperative Research and Technology Enhancement (CREATE) Act*, by Wendy H. Schacht.

[11] See CRS Report 97-104, *Manufacturing Extension Partnership Program: An Overview*, by Wendy H. Schacht.

[12] See CRS Report RL33528, *Industrial Competitiveness and Technological Advancement: Debate Over Government Policy*, by Wendy H. Schacht.

[13] See CRS Report 96-402, *Small Business Innovation Research (SBIR) Program*, by Wendy H. Schacht, and CRS Report RS22865, *The Small Business Innovation Research (SBIR) Program: Reauthorization Efforts*, by Wendy H. Schacht.

INDEX

F

J

K

L

M

N

O

P

T

U

V

W

Y

Z